PERSONAL VALUES
IN PRIMARY EDUCATION

PERSONAL VALUES IN PRIMARY EDUCATION

Norman Kirby

Harper & Row, Publishers
London

Cambridge San Francisco
Hagerstown Mexico City
Philadelphia Sao Paulo
New York Sydney

To Susan and Tim

First published in 1981
Harper & Row Ltd
28 Tavistock Street
London WC2E 7PN

British Library Cataloguing in Publication Data

Kirby, Norman
  Personal values in primary education.
  1. Education, Elementary
  I. Title
  372   LB1555

  ISBN 0-06-318130-4
  ISBN 0-06-318131-2 Pbk

Typeset by Inforum Ltd, Portsmouth
Printed and bound by the Pitman Press, Bath

CONTENTS

Acknowledgements viii
Introduction 1
Peter and the important fish 3

Chapter 1   The Best of Primary Education 6
Technological advance 8
Social change 9
Fundamental changes 11
Respect for children and their work 12
The idea that human beings are different from each other 16
Experience as the basis of learning 18
  Sensory experience 18
  Emotional experience 19
  Social experience 19
  The impact upon teaching; experience as a part of active
  learning 20
The importance of environment 21
The vital role of the teacher 25
Summary 33

Chapter 2   The Individual and the Group 35
How can individualized methods be justified? 36
  Are individualized methods the best for individuals? 36
  How are group needs to be met? 37
  Are not individualized methods, involving made-to-measure
  resources, expensive? 39

How can individualized methods be applied in practice? 39
   The individual within the group 40
      Nearness with respect 40
      Making a start 42
      A proper respect for theory 44
   If all the learning is done by the pupil, what is the role of the teacher? 45
   Does individualized teaching for thirty pupils involve thirty different lessons? 47
Can the study of groups be justified in an individualized programme? 47
   The danger of deducing general laws in education from particular cases 48
Summary 50

Chapter 3   Understanding Children 51
The middle years 54
Summary 59

Chapter 4   Some Characteristics of Children in the Middle Years 60
The desire for achievement 60
The desire to learn 65
Activity of mind, body and imagination 67
   Reality and make-believe 70
Acquisitiveness 74
   Knowing children as individuals and as members of groups 76
Summary 79

Chapter 5   The Encouraging School 81
Education in social values 81
Teaching 87
The evolving classroom 90
   Classroom organization 91
      Stage 1   Rigidity 91
      Stage 2   The beginnings of mobility 92
      Stage 3   Choices may be made 94
      Stage 4   The break-up of class teaching 95

Stage 5   The beginning of integrated or undifferentiated
           work   95
Stage 6   The ultimate in flexibility   97
Other groupings of children   99
Some patterns of organization in the teaching of reading
and mathematics   101
    Learning to read   101
    Reading for fluency   102
    Reading for comprehension   103
    Reading for pleasure   104
    Grouping according to mixed aims within the reading
    period   105
    Learning mathematics   106
Choice of learning material   107
    The knowledge explosion   120
Summary   126

Chapter 6   Concluding Remarks   128
Summary   136

References   137
Author Index   142
Subject Index   144

ACKNOWLEDGEMENTS

I owe a great debt of gratitude to Mrs. Meriel Downey who patiently read the manuscript and gave me the benefit of her own wide reading and scholarship. I am grateful for her suggestions for improving the text, and for making it possible for me to consult relevant research.

Ideas about education cannot be claimed as a private possession, and during a lifetime they come from many sources, from colleagues in the teaching profession, from children, from books, from conferences and from informal conversations.

For these many influences on my own thoughts and feelings I wish particularly to thank my colleagues and students at Goldsmiths' College, the headteachers, staff and children of schools in London, Oxfordshire, West Yorkshire and Suffolk. I regret that I cannot mention them all by name, but I should like to record here my thanks to Sue Hellier for her careful typing of the manuscript.

In the case of the children's poems appearing in the text, permission to publish them was given either by the children themselves or by the head of their school. For their contribution, too, I express my thanks.

I also thank Leslie Smith, editor of *Ideas*, for his kind permission to include, in the introduction to this book, part of an article which I wrote for that journal in 1973, on the child Peter, and for allowing me to reproduce the two mathematical tables from Derek Wheatley's article in *Ideas* (*New Era and Ideas*, Vol. 58, No. 5, 1977).

The system of education discussed in this book is that of England and Wales.

Teacher and child are referred to as he, used only as a generic term.

INTRODUCTION

This book is intended for primary students in colleges and institutes of education, and for teachers of children aged seven to eleven years in junior schools and those in middle schools in the eight to twelve age range, the middle years of childhood. Middle schools, as envisaged by the Plowden Committee, were to extend upwards 'the best of primary education', so they are here included as primary schools. In practice some middle schools follow the Plowden Committee's interpretation of the age range as eight to twelve while others with a different emphasis prefer nine to thirteen. The years referred to in this book can be considered to spread from seven to twelve, although the general principles and many of the practices could apply equally to thirteen-year-olds. Its main purpose is to direct attention to the individual at a time when self-determination is both valued and threatened, and to suggest ways in which schools can still be places where these personal values are given priority. It may therefore be of interest to teachers who seek to relate their practical work to a carefully considered philosophical approach, especially to probationary teachers, to students newly embarked on a B.Ed. course and to young persons seriously thinking about primary education as a career.

The message conveyed by the book is meant to be encouraging to the practising teacher, and optimistic, but not blindly so. A young teacher in contemporary society will soon discover that adherence to a clearly defined philosophy is not achieved without difficulty in the face of various problems encountered in the practical world of school and classroom. One lesson that has to be learned is that the day's work is not only with children but also with colleagues who may have different opinions about values. There is not consensus, even within the teaching profession, over what counts as education, a fact confirmed by the experience of teachers and the researches of sociologists (Shipman 1975). There may be problems of relationships, and demands arising from selection and standards, on the part of those who do not share his philosophy. Parents have legitimate claims, too, and it may be that their wishes are for a more traditional type of education for their children than the one offered by the young experimentally minded teacher, a situation found not only in innercity areas with a culturally mixed population, but in some outer suburbs as well. Where the children are concerned, there may be problems resulting from lack of motivation and alienation from school. On the other hand, the young teacher can surely hope to have friends and allies among those colleagues who share his views and interests, among parents who appreciate the positive approach to their children, and perhaps above all, among the children themselves who respond to the teacher's skill. Moreover, the study of education can give to the young apprentice confidence in the importance of the teacher's role.

Children's experience of state education need not be that of losing identity in the crowd, however large the school may be. The emphasis on the rights of individuals to be themselves is, of course, applicable to human beings of all ages. I remember being particularly encouraged by a visit to an East London school, not because the teaching was exceptional, but because it reflected a positive, caring attitude to children which is a familiar feature of many primary schools. No excuse is made for beginning with an apparently mundane anecdote about Peter, a slow-learning child treated by his teacher with the customary respect due to him as an individual. The urban and industrial neighbourhood of this school on the Isle of Dogs, a once busy dockland area, seemed strangely quiet and deserted, remote from the noise and bustle of Stepney on one side and Deptford on the other, but inside the school all was rich with life and colour. In one particular classroom the walls were covered with children's work and yet appeared to be uncluttered and to carry a clear message of work accomplished, so carefully had the writings and pictures been arranged. It was the spring term and that lovely season had invaded this classroom with flowers and whole branches of blossom. On this occasion the children were engaged in individual projects. Some were seated at their desks, others were moving about and a small group were clustered around their young teacher. When the latter group returned to their occupations, some of them working in pairs, the teacher moved about the room looking, listening and occasionally making suggestions. It was when she came to Peter who was sitting near me that I was able to hear their conversation.

There is nothing extraordinary about this episode. In fact most teachers would say that this is the way they behave as a matter of course. The ordinariness of the event is the reason for its inclusion here, not as a peg on which to hang a philosophy but because, in its tiny way, it sums up an attitude towards children which differs from earlier attitudes, an attitude which has been achieved as the result of years of pioneering by individuals, supported later by governmental committees, inquiries and reports, and encouraged by state provision. Another reason for mentioning individual children by name is that this everyday, caring attitude of teachers, so taken for granted, is now under threat. Economic difficulties, anxieties over standards in a world oriented towards productivity and competition, not to mention survival, the proliferation of examinations, tests and other hurdles which encourage this very spirit of competition tend to swamp the most important objective of all: the fulfilment, happiness and welfare of the individual human being.

This precious individual, however, is also a social being whose welfare depends upon other individuals. They too have rights. Although arguments are supported by reference to some of the main disciplines contributing to educational theory, this book is a personal statement of values arrived at through experience and reflection. It is largely pragmatic in its intention to reduce the distance between teacher and child in the classroom, so that even in a group of thirty children (preferably fewer!), individual children can realize their human and intellectual potential. The teacher as a creator and organizer of working groups, as well as tutor and counsellor, is seen as someone whose profession is essentially human, civilizing and worthy of respect by the community.

Peter and the important fish

Peter was busy drawing a fish and colouring it in crayon, bright green and brown. His teacher came up to him, looking carefully at his drawing. She picked it up and had a closer look. It wasn't a marvellous drawing, but Peter had spent a long time on it, totally absorbed, oblivious of everything around him.

The teacher then began asking questions about the fish, not only about its position on the paper and its colouring, but, with some imaginative speculations, about the bewildered look in its eyes. The child, alerted to a different set of thoughts about his drawing, sat up and appeared to ponder the meaning of these last remarks. He wasn't familiar with the word bewildered and tried to repeat it.

'What's bewildered, miss?'

'Puzzled.'

He tried to find reasons why the fish could be puzzled, but as he hadn't intended any such result with his simple crayoning, he hadn't much to say except to ask how and what fishes could see under water. It was obvious though that a change was taking place in Peter's attitude to his own product, considered now as something worth talking about. Questions began to flow from the child about fishes' eyes, how best to draw them, about whether fish had eyelids and whether they closed them when they went to sleep, about whether they could see what was in front, with eyes on the sides of their head, about how they could see what was coming from the front and how they knew where to go. How did they get their sense of direction? The young teacher said she did not know the answers to all these questions. She answered what she could and suggested that they consult the books in the corner and ask other people. She then considered Peter's fish as an artistic effort, coming back to her first question about its facial appearance, and discussed with him ways in which the rest of the drawing could be made to look more like water. Peter suggested putting in some bubbles and some wavy lines, and so it went on.

What is happening here? A very old situation and a very new one. Historically this is the oldest, the most primitive, the most classical teaching situation: a face-to-face meeting between a teacher and a learner. It also symbolizes certain values in primary education. Historically the threat to this situation was the intrusion of so-called class teaching: the schoolmaster, or the dame, confronted by rows of listless or rebellious children, a situation made more threatening for the teacher by the industrial revolution, payment by results, the 1870 Education Act, education for the masses, only considered profitable when the dropping of the proverbial pin could be heard.

What has been happening over the past three decades has been a return to the more genuine meeting of two minds, to conditions more likely to produce a personal relationship between teacher and child. This is what the Plowden Report of 1967 meant by the revolution in primary education.

Let us look again at Peter and the fish. The important thing is what is going on in Peter's mind, in his growing ability and willingness to learn, in his emotions, ultimately in his personality, the kind of relationship that is developing between the child and his teacher, her acceptance of him and his work and his acceptance of himself. First of all Peter may realize, intuitively rather than explicitly perhaps, that his fish is important to his teacher because she has taken the trouble to look at it, to talk about it and to use a long word about it. The fish therefore becomes important to Peter. He wants to improve upon it, to make the water look more watery, and this is the activity to which he proceeds to give attention. He was heard to repeat the word bewildered as though he liked the new sound and was trying it out. It may be stretching the educational vision too far to imagine the child adopting this new word in his everyday vocabulary, but he has obviously learned it and knows what it means. The fish has become móre than a fish: an opportunity grasped, the beginning of a relationship, a moment of growth, a fruitful experience. Language added to activity and experience spells relationship, and a burgeoning point in the education of a human being.

CHAPTER 1

THE BEST OF PRIMARY EDUCATION

It is possible to exaggerate the significance of one isolated everyday example of human behaviour, to remove it from its unremarkable, even humdrum context, and to build upon it an educational ideal of which the original agents, in this case Peter's teacher, are unaware. In the first place it would be insulting to the intelligence and the professionalism of a young teacher to assume that he invariably teaches blindly in the absence of any seriously held principles; and in the second place it would be wrong to deny that the very ease with which certain teaching styles and methods are adopted and even taken for granted today is indicative of advances having been made in educational thought and practice. At this moment in educational history, when anxieties about standards reach the stage of public debate and scapegoats are looked for, the emphasis on educational advance is important, not only to allay fear but to arrest irrational, panicked attempts to put clocks back. It is for this reason that a homely, unspectacular snapshot of Peter, a not very bright little boy with his teacher, is being used as an example of a certain quality of relationship, from which there must be no timorous turning back on the part of those who hold the governmental and above all the financial responsibilities for what goes on in schools.

Educational progress in the twentieth century has largely taken place in teachers' attitudes towards children, based both upon increased knowledge and understanding of children and their development and upon changes in society itself (Argyle 1967, Downey and Kelly 1979). Today most enlightened teachers, however modest their own pretensions to scholarship, however limited their own specialist manual or artistic skills, would, with twenty or thirty other children to think about, hope to have time to take the trouble to treat Peter as an individual person in his own right, to talk to him reassuringly on a personal level, to diagnose his particular problem and set him on the road to his own particular solution. This suggests that progress in educational thinking in the twentieth century has accelerated as a result of the acceptance of the fact of human uniqueness, leading to measures aimed at encouraging diversity rather than uniformity. Throughout the early decades of the twentieth century ways of thinking about children have led to one of the greatest revolutions in educational history, culminating in what we know as the English primary school. Yet the first intellectual steps in this direction were taken many years, even centuries ago.

It is in the context of the middle school that the Plowden Report (1967) refers to 'the best of primary education'. There is little doubt that this best is based upon vision, upon certain ways of thinking about children. But how does one get from vision to administration? How does vision become legalized? How does the inspired idea of the crank become the common practice of the state? How long does it take? The ideas upon which present-day primary education are based have been around for a very long time. Socrates believed in face-to-face dialogue. Plato believed in the importance of the learner's environment. Jesus believed in respect for the dignity of children. Rousseau believed in childhood as a period of life to be valued for its own sake. Pestalozzi believed in the value of activity and responsibility for productive work. Froebel believed in children's investigating, experimenting and finding out for themselves. Dewey believed in the idea of democracy applied to schools. Maria Montessori believed that children could be encouraged to work hard by being given the freedom to use their own initiative. Before the First World War A.S. Neill was advocating self-government, self-chosen work, opting in and opting out, based on the idea of children's responsibility and self-determination. In 1911 Edmond Holmes in *What Is and What Might Be* contrasted the current reality of the elementary school with his own vision of a new education, and in 1921 vision was given tangible shape in the founding of the New Education Fellowship. Why then did we have to wait until the second half of the twentieth century for these ideas to be put into practice on a broader scale? We know what happened to Socrates and to Jesus. Rousseau's *Émile* achieved the distinction of being the only book on education to be outrageous enough to be publicly burned. Froebelian education was outlawed from Froebel's native Prussia, and in Victorian England Charles Dickens was immortalizing the portrait of the schoolmaster as an ignorant, narrow-minded, cruel, mean, vicious, punishing pedant, while the frustrated figure of the governess moves sadly through the world of the Brontës. When one remembers that it was not until 1876 that the act was passed forbidding the employment of children under ten years old, the answer to the above question is: the time was not ripe.

With the 1931 Report of the Board of Education Consultative Committee on the Primary School (Hadow) as a watershed in educational thinking, the climate became more favourable to ideas of change. Before the first of the three Hadow Reports there were no primary schools called by that name. The word 'primary' became adopted as a result of the suggestion in the Hadow Report on the education of the adolescent (1926) that there should be separate schools, called secondary, for children over the age of eleven, and primary schools for children up to eleven years of age. It must also be remembered that the term 'elementary' continued to be used until 1944. Junior schools – a term not officially recognized until 1944 – came about almost as an afterthought.

The 1960s and some trends of thought at that time did hold some promise of a more congenial atmosphere for the growth of child-centred education. Two main developments of revolutionary importance have transformed the western scene in recent years. They are technological advance and social change.

Technological advance

To name but a few examples, the motor car and the aircraft industries have brought about greater mobility, a more diverse mixture of populations and a shrinking world. The most distant horizons have, through package holidays, become accessible to the humbler suburbs. The mass media of communication, radio, film, television and transmission by satellite have opened thoroughfares to other minds and cultures, resulting in a questioning of one's own beliefs and opinions. More destructive weapons of war have intensified the atmosphere of moral doubt and inquiry. Improved medicine, sophisticated surgery, the transplanting of organs have led to longer expectation of life, and these, together with the manufacture of drugs such as the contraceptive pill, have inevitable implications for sexual mores, marriage and divorce. Earlier marriage and longer life could mean looking at the same face over the breakfast table for seventy years, unlike the fate of many Victorian couples who married late and died in their middle years.

Social change

There has been a progressive decline in authoritarianism generally, and many historical factors have contributed to the greater confidence on the part of educators in democratic procedures. The growth of the trades union movement, efforts towards copartnership of workers and employers in industry, changes demanding a more equitable distribution of wealth after the economic upheavals of two World Wars, the emancipation of women have all pointed towards a greater say in the management of affairs by ordinary men and women. A generation of fathers who are no longer frightened of their bosses has produced a generation of children who are no longer overawed by their parents and teachers. The improved financial status of teenagers since the Second World War likewise tends to increase their independence and, with the vote at eighteen, to undermine patriarchal attitudes on the part of older people. The increasingly important part played by women in politics has meant more concern for the welfare of children. With the greater emphasis by modern educational thought on learning rather than instruction, schools and teachers have moved closer to children in more attentive, observant and friendly relationships. Social interaction between pupils and between teacher and pupil has come to be considered increasingly significant for learning. Established authorities have been having a bad time lately. On television a new era of iconoclasm and irreverence set in in the 1960s, which could perhaps be interpreted as a period of greater respect for the uninitiated, when, for example, the views of pop singers on religion were received with as much seriousness as those of archbishops. As authorities have climbed down, identifications have stepped in, and the identification of the young has generally been with their own age group.

The pluralist society is an accommodating society, one which accommodates a multitude of opinions, beliefs, cultures, traditions, religions, fashions and hair-styles. In what is known as western civilization one can believe anything and wear almost anything. This is what is called the permissive society or, more accurately, an open society with many different value systems, yet committed to the idea of human equality. With so many systems elbowing each other it is no wonder that views once held with such certainty are challenged by events. We live in an atmosphere of inquiry. Phone-in and write-in programmes on radio and television have become a technically operated kind of Speakers' Corner. More knowledge demands even more knowledge and a greater critical awareness. Patterns of occupation have changed: manual work has become mechanized and most jobs today require some critical insight. Employers want schools to produce people who are adaptable in a world where everything changes with bewildering speed. The promise of increased leisure must be met by minds open to many alternative ways of living. Choices become an everyday experience of living and therefore of learning. Such is the climate in which the visions and ideas of earlier reformers now have the opportunity to grow.

At the present time some of the greatest forward strides in educational practice have been achieved by schools inspired by the day-to-day efforts of energetic, visionary headteachers, enthusiastic teachers, parents and local authority advisers working together with a common purpose centred on children and their education. It is this attentive way of looking at children which has been the admiration of the world and attracted overseas visitors to the best of our primary schools. It is noticeable that, when visiting many of these schools, one is struck, not only by the practical versatility and aesthetic taste which have transformed the learning environment, but also by the thoughtful reference to ideas and their application to children which occurs in conversation with staff. The best of theory is surely this kind of thinking which informs practice and gives it its justification. Sometimes the theory precedes the practice and sometimes practice gives birth to new ideas and new theories. Trying out a new way of working with children leads inevitably to new ideas about children. The new ideas thus achieved may become a new theory. Added to this kind of practice-based theory is the systematic research which also goes on when new insights are gained. Normally theory and practice that go hand in hand and are interdependent are the most productive (Downey and Kelly 1979).

It is therefore not very profitable to try to determine which came first in setting the pace for the new primary schools, the theory or the practice. They are intertwined and inseparable, but in recent years the practitioners have been out in front working with children and producing a rich harvest of ideas for the research students who, themselves, are no longer in ivory towers but also trying to get to grips with the situations in school and in society at large.

It is almost impossible not to be pessimistic when considering the plight of children in present-day urban society, and experienced teachers faced with the mounting pressures and accelerating pace of social change are understandably cautious when confronted by new ideas which involve a self-inflicted, additional alteration in established practice. The following analysis is optimistic because it seeks to discover the principles underlying the 'best' as observed in varying degrees in real schools, not all of them rural and middle class, and because education itself is founded upon hope. It is a positive and not a negative concept. Even in the blackest and most daunting of human situations it enters in the guise of redemption and rehabilitation, making the most of the strengths, exploring the improvable, tapping the potential. However mistakenly interpreted or partially applied, the guiding ideas of primary education involve, not the adoption of a number of impressive novelties and ephemeral fashions, but the creation by teachers of those conditions and relationships in which individual children can learn most effectively and happily.

Fundamental changes

The most fundamental changes in primary schools have come about as a result of the application of some simple, not very new, but honestly held ideas. The following four are basic:

1 respect for children and their work,
2 the idea that human beings are different from each other,
3 experience as the basis of learning, and
4 the importance of environment, since environment is the only part of the nature-nurture duality that can be improved upon by a teacher.

Before considering where each of these key ideas might lead if taken seriously, one might think for a moment of a sensitive teacher confronted by an idea or a principle against which there can be no reasonable argument. If one believes something to be true, or rather knows it to be true, it becomes uncomfortable, to say the least, to behave as if it were not true. For example, once the fact is accepted that children are different from each other, in personality, ability and attainment, different in their interests and in their rate of learning, all sorts of traditional school rituals become anachronisms because teachers can no longer give them their allegiance and maintain professional integrity at the same time. This explains the disappearance of mass teaching, chanting of tables and mechanical reading round the class. It explains the decline of rigid timetables and the silencing of bells, and deals a death-blow to the same textbook for every child. It explains, too, the collapse of the old-fashioned project. How can one expect every child to be thrilled by coal or wool? Why should projects be any better than subjects? In fact most children of junior and middle school age are enthusiastic about history and prehistory. Many are fascinated by fossils, interested in brass-rubbing, heraldry, medieval pilgrimages and tournaments, and adore the Black Death. Likewise the idea of respect for children as fellow-workers can affect the furniture and destroy at a stroke both the teacher's desk and the notion that a classroom has a front and a back.

So in today's climate of ideas certain old practices come to be abandoned and new ones come gradually, even apprehensively, to be introduced. Obviously change does not happen overnight. In fact it is disastrous when it does. To move a whole school from an 1870 building into an open-plan building without a slow and gradual preparation in thinking, planning, experiment and practice on the part of the staff is to invite chaos.

Each of the four basic ideas mentioned above will now be examined in turn, not in the negative sense of past practices relinquished but in terms of positive directions taken.

Respect for children and their work

Human relationships are central to the work of a school. People are its main concern and organizational policies are only ancillary to this purpose and therefore derivative. Optimism born of the faith in children and in their ability to learn, given the encouragement of good teachers and favourable environmental conditions, reflects a greater faith in educability in general. This belief in the potential of children is applied also in the education of the slow learner and of the handicapped child. There is a firm conviction among teachers that children are capable of much more achievement and higher standards of work than was ever thought possible before, with the result that children are given more freedom to learn, more choices and materials with which to operate and more space in which to move. Closer observation of children has led to their being allowed greater responsibility for their own learning, and more opportunities to pursue their own interests. According to R.S. Peters (1966), people can only become persons in a society which respects their dignity as self-determining agents, capable of making moral choices and decisions, and, with this same respect applied to children, he argues that they will only develop as persons in so far as they learn to think of themselves as such. Their opinions must be listened to and their idiosyncrasies considered rather than ridiculed. Positive criticism of children's behaviour is consistent with the view of children as people who are learning self-respect along with the acceptance of responsibility for their own actions (Hirst and Peters 1970). In a climate of work where each person is valued and receives unconditional acceptance, individuals come to accept each other and appreciate each other's work (Downey 1977). The teacher, though still the source of security and authority, is no longer the only one from whom to gain recognition. With authoritarianism in decline, democratic techniques are meaningless without the true democracy which is founded upon mutual respect. The truly democratic classroom is a centre of 'infection' in which children catch their enthusiasms and interests and standards from the teacher and from each other. The value placed upon the individual person is due in part to the fact that every person is unique, and not only responds to teaching in a unique and personal way, but also has a unique contribution to make. Respect for children's work is a corrective both to the old-fashioned view that education is all right for children so long as they don't like it, and the laissez-faire view that equates education with amusement or aimless activity. In a good school children develop standards from within which may be far higher than any externally imposed standards. They set themselves problems which lead to an endless search for knowledge, and develop skills which heighten their perceptions and refine their sensitivities. The practical experience of teachers who have worked successfully in this way has led to great changes in the attitudes of teachers towards children. Work proceeds according to the principle of respect for the individual, as a result of which new light is shed upon child nature and attitudes become modified still further.

It may be conceded that respect for the child's product is justifiable, on motivational grounds, in the spheres of practical, physical and artistic skills, but that in the area of 'academic' seriousness, junior children have nothing to contribute to the 'higher' levels of reasoning. Yet most thinking is an exploration of experience, and each phase of development prefigures the next, earlier with some children, later with others. Teachers who value children's present thinking and take it seriously are constantly discovering that some of the investigations carried out by juniors could rightly be called academic and foreshadow the researches of older students. This potential strength, so often underestimated or disregarded, and therefore prevented from developing (because 'they are not old enough'), often comes to light whenever children living in an atmosphere of inquiry and experiment are given freedom and time for discussion, though it would be irresponsible to respect everything a child produces; some of it might not reach his own standards.

A group of eight-year-old children, to whom I was attempting to teach history, were looking at a reproduction of the Bayeux Tapestry. They had enjoyed stories of the deeds of various invaders of Britain, beginning with the Romans, following with the Angles, Saxons and Jutes, and then the Danes. They had reached a new stage in our island's history with the year 1066 and were ready for the coming of the Normans. They had then been told the story of Harold's shipwreck, his rescue and reception at the court of Duke William of Normandy, and of his promise to the Duke, of the death of Edward the Confessor, of the problem of a successor, of the choice made by the Witan and of the Battle of Hastings. The children were familiar with the armour and equipment of the English, having seen pictures and also having been to the Tower of London, and were able to appreciate the differences between their shorter tunics, round helmets and shields and the longer coats of mail and more protective helmets and shields of the Normans. After a few minutes' study of the picture a boy remarked, 'There aren't any English in the picture.' The other children, looking more closely, were unable to detect what they had come to think of as English helmets and tunics and shields. Another boy said, 'Where are the English?' A third replied, 'Here is Harold, because he's got an arrow in his eye.' A fourth boy objected, 'But he's wearing Norman armour. Look, he's got a helmet with a nose-piece and a long coat of mail.' The teacher then asked, 'Why do they all look like Normans?' The suggestions which followed from the children were both enlightening and amusing. One boy, who was particularly interested in stories of the Second World War, suggested that the English had a fifth column whom they dressed up as Normans so that they could penetrate the enemy ranks as spies. This contribution was not acceptable to the group: 'They didn't have spies in those days.' 'Yes they did. Hereward the Wake was given away by a spy.' Another solution was offered by a girl who asked tentatively, 'Fashions are supposed to come from France, aren't they?' When answered in the affirmative she went on, 'Well the Normans lived in France, and the English preferred to wear the French fashions.' This explanation was greeted with mild derision, especially by the boys in the group. Then another girl, who had obviously been thinking hard all this time, and in spite of the poor reception given to the previous speaker's offering, was put on to the most likely track by the thought of French ladies and their needlework, volunteered the following reasoning: 'You said that the tapestry was supposed to have been woven by ladies at the court of Duke William in Normandy. Well perhaps they had never travelled to England and didn't know what the English looked like, so they just made pictures of the soldiers they knew.' The group felt that this was the most reasonable explanation offered hitherto and later reference to books and consultation with more learned historians tended to support the child's hunch.

One boy grumbled, 'Trust a woman not to know anything about soldiers.' Elizabeth, the last girl contributor to the discussion, sprang to the defence of her sex by saying, 'You only know because you've had lessons on it. If you're so clever why don't you try to do better than the women of Normandy?' 'What do you mean?' the boy asked. 'Well you're supposed to know what the English soldiers looked like at the Battle of Hastings. Why don't you do your own Bayeux Tapestry instead of criticizing?' This remark which was only meant as a taunt was seized upon by the whole group as an opportunity. 'Oh sir, couldn't we all do that? Please!'

From a situation such as this a number of paradoxical thoughts spring to mind: firstly, the importance of having the patience to listen to children, and not having prespecified objectives so that the teacher would have the opportunity to use any unexpected outcomes as important teaching points (Hogben 1972). Secondly is the value of 'ignorance' on the part of the teacher, leading him to ask a real question of his pupils so that all can enjoy the joint enterprise of searching for the truth. An intellectual investigation in partnership with an educated adult on equal terms can surely be an invaluable educative experience for any child. As Barnes (1976) and Stubbs (1976) point out, much time is spent by teachers asking closed questions, to which they already know the answers, resulting in what Stubbs terms 'pseudo-dialogue'. Thirdly, there is the positive contribution to discussion that can be made even by a wild guess, a hypothesis putting another member of the group on to the scent of the most likely approximation to the truth. Fourthly to be mentioned is the intellectual and social value of shared speculation itself (referred to by Barnes as exploratory thinking), whether or not the factual truth is arrived at. Fifthly, there follows the opportunity afforded by such an arousal of group interest to continue the investigation further, to look up references, to consult authorities and to visit libraries. Finally, one cannot ignore the immense worth of a socially relaxed climate in which such discussions and exchanges of opinion can take place, where children fear neither censure not ridicule.

Consideration of such a small classroom incident as this leads us to reflect upon the weighty issue of indoctrination and uncritical acceptance of whatever one is told by an authority, be it parent, teacher or mass media. One only has to listen to children who have been given the freedom to discuss their intellectual problems to be convinced that the only way to develop a critical faculty is by using it.

That incident marked the beginning of a series of periods in which the children, using reference books and pictures, painted a frieze depicting the main events of that time, from the shipwreck of Harold to the coronation of William I, and the burning of houses in London by Norman soldiers. For this last part of the frieze a group of boys carefully copied pictures of English houses, then proceeded to smear them with red paint to depict fire issuing from doors and windows. The frieze went round three walls of the classroom and was an indication of the children's aesthetic and intellectual achievement.

Associated with the principle of respect for children and their work is the second of the four fundamental ideas which have helped to produce primary education at its best.

The idea that human beings are different from each other

On the one hand we are indebted to Freud and Erikson who have highlighted the origins and importance of individual differences in personality and affective response; on the other to Piaget and Bruner who recognize children's intellectual or cognitive development as unique. We know from their work that children neither develop at the same rate nor reach limits predetermined by genetic factors.

We find then that arising out of this one crucial idea of individual differences come such modern developments as flexibility in teaching methods and in groupings of children. At the outset it must be firmly stated that, where the organization of schools and classrooms and teaching procedures are concerned, psychological considerations are primary and basic; such things as methods and groupings are of secondary importance and subject to change.

Consideration for individual differences in ability means individual attention (which should draw the attention of the responsible authorities to the need for smaller and more manageable classes), more freedom for the child to learn in his own way, while the close observation of children's differing interests has led to the provision of varied materials for work, the exercise of choice (and this involves responsibility) and appropriate space in which to work. Consequently this means a certain amount of mobility, moving into a suitable work area, for example, from the reading corner to the practical work corner. If teachers are to help individual children and see what is going on, this could entail knocking down a wall, in other words an open-plan classroom. So building design is also affected.

But if buildings as well as teachers are to be child-centred, one should spare a thought for one very marked characteristic of human beings at any age: the childhood wish to be secure, encircled, safe in a hidy-hole under the stairs or in the attic, unassailable in a tree house with the rope ladder pulled up, out of reach of the ravages of neighbouring gangs, secure in a camp in the bushes or in a wooden shack, secure in a room with a teacher and a story and the door closed. That is why most (but not all) open-plan schools have provision for quiet rooms where children can withdraw. The better ones provide some kind of home base which children can call their own and where they can keep their belongings.

Because teachers, too, differ from each other in their gifts and interests, a change in staff relationships is one sign of the acknowledgement that no teacher can know it all, that in a changing world the most urgent task is to encourage the spirit of inquiry among pupils. For teachers this might mean using each other as well as other adults and children as a team in the search for knowledge. At the primary level in a warm-hearted school, collaboration between teachers and between children and all adults in the school is not so much a formal organization as an informal way of life, part of the school's ethos. The idea of inter-related learning arises not only from the nature and apprehension of knowledge itself but also from these social considerations.

Because children learn at different speeds, the use of time also demands greater adaptability. Differing interests not only presuppose variety in the provision of materials, but require allowances to be made for greater involvement in an interest and time to pursue it without interruption. There should always be time to do worthwhile things. Respect for children is again involved here in the time allowed for an individual who is becoming more and more deeply absorbed in a solitary piece of work. It is not the number of things done in a day that matters, but the depth and intensity and concentration with which each thing is done. Different rates of learning and the encouragement given to different interests could therefore lead imperceptibly to the idea of the undifferentiated day – imperceptibly, because timetables, like buildings, cannot be transformed overnight. A bell used to ring audibly in the corridor to signify a change of activity. (Could a mere bell ever be expected to signify the death of one interest and the birth of another?) Then it rang inaudibly inside the teacher's head. Now it is being encouraged to ring inside the child's head. A teacher in this context would find difficulty in saying 'Don't interrupt my lesson'. Whose lesson is it?

Experience as the basis of learning

The next potent idea dates back at least as far as the eighteenth century, to the empirical philosophy of John Locke: that experience, and particularly sensation, is the basis of learning. Since then this theory has been underlined by psychological research, by investigations into human perception, learning and concept formation, and by studies in child development. Modern psychology supported the earlier philosophy by emphasizing that before learning could take place its subject matter must make an organic connection with what the child had already experienced, or, in Piaget's terms (Piaget 1950, 1952), there must be assimilation of the new and accommodation by the old (the existing mental structures). Again individual differences are involved. Experience of life varies from one child to another, so learning has to be assimilated in a multitude of different patterns. This gives additional support to the demand for an individual and flexible approach on the part of the teacher. When one starts with the idea of personal experience as the foundation of learning, then certain other things follow which have an impact on methods, curriculum, building, equipment, furniture, materials and organization.

Sensory experience

Experience includes sensory, emotional and social experience. A primary school teacher will need to know his pupils in order to use adequately and develop appropriately each child's individual experience, and will add new individual and group experiences, gathering easily accessible concrete objects and a great variety of materials. Efficient recordkeeping by the teacher is important not only as a reminder of children's progress and potentialities, but as an indicator of appropriate provision for developing work and ideas related to the circumstances and needs of individuals.

An understanding of the fundamental nature of physical experience in its functional and expressive aspects leads to the development of freer techniques of acquiring all forms of bodily and motor skills in movement and physical education.

Emotional experience

The importance of a child's emotional life as the foundation of his intellectual development means at least two preoccupations for the teacher: (a) an emphasis on secure personal relationships within the school, implying acceptance of the contribution of each to the life and work of the whole, and (b) greater prominence in primary education given to the expressive arts, to drawing and painting in tune with the insights and feelings of children, to drama, dance, music and literature (Sinclair de Zwart 1969, Jones 1972). Faith in children's creative response to the arts as a starting point for their educational development has been demonstrated by A.L. Stone (1949) with the teaching of movement and by Sybil Marshall (1963) using visual art. The best of the primary schools are rich in children's art work, remarkable for sensitive drawings of leaves, twigs and insects, rubbings upon bark, brass or wood, for simple pottery, needlework and weaving, and lino-cuts in subtle, sombre or glowing colours. The cognitive side of learning is not the only concern of teachers of younger children.

Social experience

Where social experience is concerned, it has been found that, in the friendlier, democratic climate of the school, children learn from each other regardless of age or ability. With experience as the basis of learning, age becomes less relevant, except for the convenience of administration, and so vertical (or 'family') grouping is a feature of some present-day primary schools. There are moments when adults and children can enjoy an experience as equals: the arrival of an unfamiliar bird on the bird table, the sight of a dragonfly hatching out, planting a tree in a London playground. Where human relationships are a basic concern in education the way is open for such developments as nonstreaming, self-chosen groupings and groups based on friendship.

The acceptance of school as part of the community throws into relief the importance of the aspirations of parents. Their participation and that of other adults in the life and work of the school is now welcomed as an essential ingredient in the social development of the children. The community school is another innovation. For example, in 1975 a community education centre was opened on the site of a former I.C.I. chemical waste tip in Manchester. It consists of two comprehensive schools, a college of further education, an adult education centre, a recreation complex, a district library, an old people's centre, a 250-seat theatre and seven dining rooms. There is a crèche for the youngest children while their mothers attend adult classes, and primary school children use the swimming pool. There is much sharing of accommodation and facilities. Dining rooms, leisure centre, library, school hall and woodwork shop are used by adults and children who, because they are in a public place, like any other citizens, should not think that education is in some way separate from 'real life'. At Liverpool, also, a national centre for Urban Community Education has grown out of the Liverpool Educational Priority Area Project (Midwinter 1974).

The impact upon teaching: experience as a part of active learning

The change from didactic methods to more active learning is an important development bound up with the emphasis upon experience, and dates back at least to as long ago as the Hadow Report on primary education (1931).

In the years immediately following the Second World War there was a widespread interest in activity methods, mixed with a certain amount of confusion about the meaning of the term and its application in the classroom. A popular book at this time was *Activity in the Primary School*, by M.V. Daniel (1947). One remarkable and all-too-common practice in some schools was to enter Activity on the timetable as a separate subject.

Oral teaching can still be thought of as an important part of education, with listening given its rightful place as a valuable and enjoyable activity, but its character is changing from a formal set-piece, punctuated by questions and answers, to something more like natural conversation. Lessons are not 'delivered' in a special 'teacher's voice' but follow the easy rhythm of talk between friends. Questions are becoming inspirational rather than inquisitorial, leading to open-ended speculation and further investigation rather than to prescribed right answers. In fact the measure of a teacher's success can be valued more in terms of the quality of the children's questions than the rightness of their answers (Barnes 1976, Stubbs 1976). The offering of choice is an important factor in the encouragement of individuality and independence. This allows children to take the initiative and participate actively in their own learning. In a world equipped with more widespread, powerful and subtle weapons in the service of indoctrination, teachers have come to realize that the only way to develop rational thought is by having early practice in learning how to think. Though the ideas put forward in the Hadow Report were slow to be applied in practice, there were more and more schools in the 1940s where formulation of ideas was done by children after observation and discovery rather than by the teacher beforehand (Marshall 1963). More opportunities are now given for the exercise of imagination, in mathematics as well as in art, and there is more freedom for each child to satisfy his natural curiosity by first-hand experiment: building a weather station, measuring the height of a tree, plotting the path of a stream, making a map of sounds in the country or of smells in the town, brass-rubbing in the local church, making musical instruments, writing original verses, working out plays in small groups, trying out new improvisations in movement. These and a host of similar activities, together with the regular learning and exercise of skills, would fit naturally into a present-day curriculum. In those earlier decades primary school teachers were learning the arts of compromise, learning to be opportunists, to pick up every chance experience which might lead to the development of an interest: the swarm of bees which suddenly arrived in a London school playground, a surprise encounter with exotic foreign visitors, the hatching out of a dragonfly. Teachers were learning, too, to balance their class teaching with group and individual work. Activity obviously includes taking in as well as giving out: reading good literature, listening to stories and poetry, learning to enjoy good music, being exposed to beauty of form in works of art and in the design of objects in the environment were all seen as indispensable parts of a child's education.

Today many of the topics studied in some primary schools are self-chosen by the pupils. Situations are created in which children are eager to learn. The three Rs are not always envisaged as a preliminary task in preparation for more meaningful experiences later, but as necessary and relevant work arising from interesting experiences *now*. Practice periods then fall naturally into place.

The importance of environment

Linked with the many studies of children and their development, particularly in connection with investigations into the causes of delinquency and backwardness, there has been an ever-increasing volume of work done on the effect of environment upon children's achievement and behaviour (Douglas 1964).

Putting into practice the idea of the environment as inseparable from the child's experience explains a number of present-day trends, including the provision and use of many diverse, individual and group experiences originating from the environment, the creation of deliberate links with the neighbourhood of people and things and learning how to use local resources. Environmental and field studies and school journeys encourage methods of investigation and experiment, the use of special staff abilities and inter-related subject matter.

Since much research in the 1950s and 1960s showed the effects of social class upon scholastic achievement (Little and Westergaard, 1964, Banks, 1968), school came to be seen as a place that might compensate for inequalities of social environments (Plowden 1967). Compensatory experiences in so-called priority areas included increased opportunities for the development of language, especially speech, the provision of books and a rich supply of varied materials, but, as Bernstein (1968) points out, such educational measures, good as they are in themselves, cannot compensate for society. Another criticism of compensatory education from a different angle is that its emphasis can all too easily be upon the negative aspects of a child's environment, and it can ignore the opportunities afforded to children by urban life.

The mass media are rightly full of examples of children at the mercy of hostile and destructive environments. It is undeniable that children do suffer from many features of urban living, the noise, the ugliness, the lack of privacy, but in one respect this all too familiar picture ignores an important characteristic of children themselves. Undoubtedly they are victims, but they are also creators. They fight back, sometimes in negative ways, through destruction, vandalism and rebellion against adult authority, but they also respond to their surroundings positively by interacting with it as a partner in their own purposes: in constructive and dramatic play, in making collections, in explorations of local landmarks, in helping people in their neighbourhood and in caring for creatures. As Bernstein has indicated, compensatory education has serious limitations, and it would be hypocritical and insensitive to deny this, but there are varied ways in which teachers, who are also environmental casualties, can work with children to produce a positive and creative environment in school. They can play a vital role in helping children to look at their surroundings imaginatively, and always with an active response in mind. Children can catch the teacher's enthusiasm for interesting objects and his concern for high standards in presenting them. The care with which their own work is presented back to them in a sensitive display is rewarded by an extension of their interests and an improvement of their own output. The children's creative abilities are fostered by input, by feeding in a rich variety of visual patterns, remembered and selected as a result of close, involved observation of natural and man-made materials. Other abilities, too, are stimulated into growth by carefully planned displays. The ability to classify can develop when children are busy arranging together objects which have something in common. Language skills, in both speech and writing, are seen to grow when children take part in discussions based on displays which they then supplement with artistic, scientific and written work of their own. New interests can be aroused by a simple but dramatic presentation of objects. The grasping of relationships, so important for intellectual development, can be reinforced by the uncluttered arrangement of a group of objects related in various ways. The best objects for display are the natural, inexpensive, basic materials with quiet, subtle colours and plain backgrounds, as a corrective to the usually garish ones by which many children are confronted in the commercial world of comics and supermarkets. Objects on different levels, contrasting shapes and textures, angles which make for alternating light and shade lend variety to a display, but there should be a unity in the presentation so that attention is focused rather than dissipated. All displays should have an educational purpose, whether it be to sharpen the perceptions or more overtly to lead to action, whether it be touching and handling or further investigation, talking, reading and writing. Children's work can be shown sharing the honours with adult works of art. This is educative in itself, and a great boost to a child's self-confidence.

With few exceptions, no place in school is too small or too large to house an inspiring display, from the odd nooks and crannies to the large hall with its high ceiling, and the entrance foyer where the head, with a suitable array of well-chosen materials, can set a standard and establish a tasteful, welcoming atmosphere not only for visitors but for his staff and children as well. One important result of such efforts is respect for materials and craftsmanship. Boldness and simplicity rather than stylishness are the characteristics of a good display.

Whereas the country child is privileged by easy access to objects of

natural beauty, some twentieth-century environments are niggardly providers of visual delights, and the less fortunate town child in his concrete
jungle is hard pressed to find anything upon which his eye can rest with any
pleasure. While it is hypocritical to talk of compensatory experiences when
nothing short of a housing revolution will solve this problem, teachers
might nevertheless welcome ideas which, imaginatively adapted to their
own situation, can help them to begin with children the task of creating a
more acceptable environment within the school (Jarman 1972).

Granted the element of deprivation and exile from their natural birthright
endured by children in some urban environments, are there not a few
compensations for living at the heart or on the fringe of a big city: the wide
variety of people and jobs, the greater number of opportunities for human
contact and conversation, more movements and groups to be involved with,
the old and the young, the familiar and the foreign, shops of all descriptions,
sizes and nationalities, arts and entertainments unglimpsed by those living
further out, more occasions to be grasped, not fewer but different adventures? What is more exciting, a camp in the bracken or a hut made of petrol
tins behind the advertisement hoardings, a swing attached to a tree or one
tied to a lamp-post? Children, it seems, inhabit a child's world wherever
they are, and fashion it according to fantasy, imagination and heart's desire.
But is imagination starved by so much of man's handiwork? To look at some
urban developments one might be tempted to think so, yet to observe
children is to see them using what they have got, be it apparently ever so
little. In these eventualities a teacher may come to the rescue, not to shatter
the child's own world with prearranged projects but with a wealth of ideas
and practical activities to extend what might otherwise be a limited horizon,
or to make complexities meaningful. Work might start from the family with
its many varied occupations and individual histories, the structure, heating,
lighting and plumbing of the house, and venture out into the neighbourhood in an exhaustive plan of activities inspired by the streets, the shops,
the world of work and the occasional wildlife.

The teacher makes use of the environment as a starting point, starts from
where the children are but does not stay there. Modern technology has
supplied additional extensions of experience through new media: film,
television, tape-recorder and teaching machine, and there are many new
approaches to mathematics and science using the man-made as well as the
natural environment. In the light of technological expansion in the world at
large, schools have had to come to terms with the fact that knowledge itself

quickly becomes obsolete. Adaptability to change is necessary for survival. In such a time of upheaval another question arises. It is conceivable that children could suffer more from overstimulation than from the lack of stimulation in our contemporary multisensational environment. This is particularly true in densely populated areas where traffic provides a background of almost continuous noise and in homes where the television is switched on day and night.

Indiscriminate, unselected stimulation can amount to another kind of deprivation. A general level of conversation amounting to a noise directed to no one in particular, instead of talk directed personally, specifically and positively to a child, makes it difficult for any child to develop habits of attention. Joan Tough (1973, 1977) shows how children from homes where little real conversation goes on and where they are not listened to come to school apparently linguistically retarded; one of their main problems is that they have never had the opportunity to practise speech because no one has listened seriously to them or responded sensitively to their interests and concerns.

On the positive side of this picture some teachers aim at kinds of stimulation that challenge a child to respond. If stimulation is too novel on the one hand or too familiar on the other, there is no challenge and no response. In Bruner's view cognitive growth is directly linked with the child's interaction with the environment, a process most profitably fostered by the intervention of a teacher who arouses his pupils to action and to speech as the means to acquire concepts. The child is not left to the mercy of the environment, in a hit or miss fashion, because the teacher is there to provide the opportunities for activity, mental and linguistic as well as physical, and to structure the experiences upon which conceptual development depends. There has to be a happy medium between too much novelty and too much familiarity of experience which the practised teacher can sense intuitively. So when it comes to the rich environment in the classroom and the stimulating choices offered to children in primary schools, it must be remembered that it is the teacher who starts with an act of choice. First of all, the choices offered to the children are within their own range. To some extent they are circumscribed. They are certainly not haphazard.

The vital role of the teacher

The foregoing description of life in some English primary schools may appear idealistic, but after all this is meant to be a true account of the 'best in

Primary Education'. One underlying emphasis should be noticeable: that the quality of the teacher is the one essential, constant feature in the success of any educational system, whether groupings are vertical or horizontal, whether buildings are of glass and steel or mud and thatch, whether communication is by television and tape-recorder or blackboard and slate. With or without material resources, the one indispensable ingredient of a sound education is the personal intervention of a good teacher in the life of a child. Because children responded so positively to the new approaches, bringing many surprises and unexpected achievements, teachers have come to accept the element of unpredictability, which is an inevitable counterpart to the open-ended individual approach, as a source of surprise and delight not previously enjoyed by the teacher who 'knew all the answers'.

Among the positive responses it can be stated that the range of achievement in mathematics and science is in advance of what it was twenty years ago. In an analysis of mathematical tests carried out at different times during the present century, Wheatley (1977) presents a comparison between the demands made upon children in conceptual and linguistic achievement by certain tests of mathematical attainment carried out in 1937, 1948 and 1962 (the Essex Tests) and the 1976 TAMS Tests (Testing of Attainment in Mathematics Survey), produced by the National Foundation for Educational Research. There is a striking contrast between the narrow limitations of the three earlier tests, with their concern for computational skills, and the richness of the 1976 tests, more occupied with understanding of a wide variety of concepts. It is undeniable that, according to the tables published in this article, the number of mathematical concepts and mathematical terms with which children in 1976 were expected to be familiar shows that the mathematical content has been greatly extended since those earlier decades.

In the changed climate of knowledge of the development of mathematical thinking in children (Piaget 1952), this is understandable. According to Choat (1978, 1980) the tendency to equate mathematics with arithmetic ignores the extent to which the whole of life, from the child's earliest experiences, is permeated with mathematical content, significance and activity.

Summarizing the tables reproduced in Wheatley's article, the total number of mathematical concepts tested was 16 in 1937, 16 in 1948, 16 in 1962, and 37 in 1976 in the TAMS test. Where mathematical language is concerned the tables reveal that the number of different mathematical

TABLE 1: MATHEMATICAL CONCEPTS

	1937	1948	1962	TAMS
Addition of Number	*	*	*	*
Subtraction of Number	*	*	*	*
Multiplication of Number	*	*	*	*
Division of Number	*	*	*	
Addition of Money		*		*
Subtraction of Money	*			*
Multiplication of Money	*	*	*	*
Division of Money	*	*		
Addition of Measurements				*
Subtraction of Measurements	*			
Multiplication of Measurements		*	*	
Division of Measurements		*	*	
Area (Rectangles)	*	*	*	
Circumference	*	*	*	
Vulgar Fractions	*	*		
Decimal Fractions	*			*
Long Multiplication		*	*	
Long Division	*	*	*	
Problems Involving Time	*	*	*	*
Relationships — Number	*		*	*
Proportional Relationships	*		*	*
Speed			*	
Unequal Division		*	*	*
Ability To Read a Graph (Block)				*
Series of Numbers				*
Volume				*
Ordinal Numbers				*
Size of Angles				*
Timetables				*
24-Hour Clock				*
Flow Diagram				*
Place Value				*
Nets and 3D Shapes				*
Probability				*
Understanding of 4 Rules				*
Plans				*
Scales — Scale Drawing				*
Use of Brackets				*
Equations				*
Mapping				*
Area of Shapes Other Than Rectangle				*
Symmetry				*
Percentage (very simple)				*

	1937	1948	1962	TAMS
Understanding of vulgar and decimal fractions				*
Plotting				*
Compass Points				*
Reading a Pie Chart				*
Reading a Conversion Graph				*
CONCEPTS TESTED	16	16	16	37

TABLE 2: MATHEMATICAL LANGUAGE

	1937	1948	1962	TAMS
Add	*	*		
Take	*			
Subtract	*			
Divide	*	*	*	
Share	*			
Times		*		*
Multiply	*	*	*	
Cost	*	*	*	*
How Many	*	*	*	*
How Much	*	*	*	*
Oblong	*		*	
Rectangle		*		
Difference	*		*	
Width	*	*	*	
Length	*	*	*	*
Square	*		*	*
Area	*	*	*	*
Equally	*			*
Reduce		*		
One-half		*		
Younger Than		*		
Bill		*	*	
Average		*		
Twice		*		
Longer Than			*	*
Sum of			*	*
Large			*	*
Smaller			*	*
Whole Number			*	
Remainder			*	
Late			*	*
Time			*	
Diagram			*	*
Speed			*	
Size				*

Shape				*
Big				*
Percentage				*
Fraction				*
Short				*
Tall				*
Graph				*
Chart				*
Same				*
Parallelogram				*
Cube				*
Sixth				*
Estimate				*
Angles				*
Degrees				*
Diagrams				*
Arrows				*
Net				*
Cylinder				*
Distance				*
Proportion				*
Decimal				*
Plan				*
Wide				*
Statement				*
Solid				*
Cone				*
Cuboid				*
Cylinder				*
Pyramid				*
Sphere				*
Set				*
Direction (NE)				*
Pie Chart				*
Convert				*
Equation				*
Scale				*
MATHEMATICAL WORDS				
TOTALS	16	17	22	52

words used in the tests was 16 in 1937, 17 in 1948, 22 in 1962, and 52 in the 1976 TAMS test.

To take a few examples, such concepts as volume, the size of angles, place value, probability, scales and scale drawing, equations, the area of shapes other than the rectangle, symmetry, simple percentages, the understanding of vulgar and decimal fractions, compass points and the ability to read a block graph, all included among other concepts in the 1976 test, do not appear in 1937, 1948 or 1962. The words percentage, fraction, decimal, graph, chart, parallelogram, estimate, angles, degrees, proportion, cylinder, cube, pyramid, sphere, equation, scale, used among other words in the 1976 test, are absent from the three earlier tests.

On the other side of the coin, long division and long multiplication, and the words divide and multiply, present in the earlier tests, are absent from the TAMS test. A more recent survey carried out in 1978 by the government's Assessment of Performance Unit on attainment in mathematics, with a representative sample of 13,000 children from 1,000 schools, has tended to show that most pupils can do simple sums and can handle the mechanics of mathematics, but have difficulty when asked to apply these skills to everyday problems. It would be premature to interpret these latest findings in the light of the amount of emphasis placed by teachers in the 1970s upon basic knowledge, and tempting to ascribe the results, as their American counterparts have done in a similar survey (1979), to the 'back to the basics' movement and to too much attention to drills at the expense of problem-solving.

Another report which underlines the risks involved in hasty interpretation of results is that by Neville Bennett on teaching styles and pupil progress (1976). In the analyses of the different progress of pupils in different kinds of teaching styles it was found that, in the basic subjects, formal methods were the most effective. In the same research it was also found that one of the best teachers was one in the informal category whose work was well organized and clearly structured. It appeared, too, that to teach well informally was more difficult than to teach well formally. More was required of the teacher in the careful structuring of activities with an emphasis on the cognitive content of the work when the atmosphere was one of informality.

Results, so far published, of a long-term study of primary education by the Oracle team at Leicester University (Galton, M. et al. 1980), based on observation, suggest that the traditional curriculum, with its emphasis on the basic skills of language and mathematics, still occupies a central place in primary school practice. Support for the broad curriculum of the primary school is also given by Her Majesty's Inspectors in their survey of English primary schools (1978), which shows that achievement in tests of basic reading and mathematics was highest among those children who studied a wide range of topics, using a wide variety of approaches. They warn that narrow concentration on basic skills, by restricting the range of work, could even damage those very skills.

The keywords to successful learning, according to the Oracle project, are active attention and involvement on the part of the children, and research by Neville Bennett (Bennett 1976) shows that the most important determinant of achievement in a topic is the amount of time in which children are actively engaged in the work. Great emphasis in all this research is placed on the role of the teacher in selecting topics appropriate to children, raising the level of interest and provoking their thought. The concept of activity is seen to be a demanding one, involving the responsibility of the child, and essentially dependent for its effectiveness on the quality of the teacher.

Much research in the 1970s has been devoted to analysis of the positive uses of school time, measured in terms of pupils' grasp of opportunities for learning; and in those areas in which success in education is amenable both to definition and to measurement such studies are necessary and give insights into the complex processes of teaching. The primary school tradition, without ignoring or neglecting its function to promote learning, has recognized the value of time devoted to many different aspects of a child's life: to fostering relationships, developing a concept of self and of morality, using interests to promote habits of voluntary attention, encouraging communication and discussion, creating a love of literature and the arts, delight in physical skills, reverence for living creatures, enjoyment of the natural environment, and a number of other unquantifiable values, including time for play. These are considerations with some bearing on cognitive as well as social and emotional development (Choat 1978, Eisner 1979). Research into learning has come a long way in the twentieth century, but, in our detailed analyses of school activities, we are still far from being able to evaluate their significance for each child who experiences them. Researchers themselves are clearly aware of the limitations of observation in yielding accurate knowledge of the learner's processes (Raban et al. 1976) and in shedding light on all the complexities of teaching. Qualitative as well as quantitative factors need to be considered (Berliner 1976, Hamilton and Delamont 1974). Objective analysis must somehow be balanced by subjective experience where issues so complex as teaching and learning are concerned. Piaget's great contribution to research is the degree of insight his work gives into learning experienced as well as observed.

From the children's point of view the 1960s, for those schools wedded to the four principles referred to above, were the golden age of primary education. Respect for children, both as persons and as producers of work, as craftsmen and artists, acknowledgement, in practical terms, of their uniqueness and their ability to learn in their own way, recognition of the value of their experience as a starting point for their education and concern for the environment in which they grew affected different teachers and schools in different ways. These ideas meant greater value placed upon individual differences and a corresponding emphasis upon the encouragement of diversity and self-expression. This was evident not only in the arts but in basic skills, notably mathematics, as well. Linguistic as well as artistic products were bolder and more versatile. Creativity became a key word in areas as diverse as those of science and physical education. School was thought of as a stimulating, imaginative and encouraging environment. This was the period when overseas visitors came over in large numbers to study and to admire the English primary school.

Not all teachers were successful with the new approach. There were those, on the one hand, who felt that what they had imagined to be their own particular gifts, for example, of exposition, instruction and demonstration, had become devalued, and on the other, those who went overboard in a superficial acceptance of letting children do as they liked.

Recent research has tended to restore the confidence of teachers in a more positive role without negating the advances made in the understanding of children (Flanders and Simon 1969, Rosenshine 1971, Gage 1972, Dunkin and Biddle 1974). Interaction Analysis, a system of analysis of classroom behaviour devised by Flanders to study teacher effectiveness, aims to provide a tool for student teachers to gain insights into their own teaching. It is generally acknowledged – if it was ever in doubt – that children need teachers, and teachers, according to McNamara and Desforges, need an applied knowledge of teaching centred in the classroom, and based on research (McNamara and Desforges 1978).

To adopt any so-called new approach, for example, the integrated day, vertical grouping, team teaching, the open-plan classroom, without the basic philosophy of a risk-taking trust in children and a firm belief in the educative power of human relationships, and in particular the child's relationship with a teacher who responds rather than merely reacts, is to choose the by-product rather than the essence, the side-effect rather than the cause, the outer clothing rather than the inner spirit.

All four fundamental changes outlined above relate to the value placed upon the child as an individual person and to his right to receive an education appropriate to his needs. Let us reiterate the importance of the following:

1 Respect for the child implies recognition of the unique, unrepeatable identity of each human being.
2 Acknowledgement of human diversity emphasizes the individual character of each person and the personal qualities which distinguish him from others.
3 Experience belongs to the individual.
4 Likewise environment, apprehended, suffered and enjoyed in ways peculiar to the individual, has, together with heredity, helped to make him the unique person he is.

It is not surprising then that progress in education in the present century has been towards reducing the distance between teacher and learner both psychologically in personal relationships and physically and temporally in the details of organization and administration. It has meant moving in the direction of a more intimate knowledge of individual children and an orientation towards a more sympathetic understanding of their life-styles and problems. In practice this has resulted in increased individualization of work in school and a gradual evolution of classroom procedures, directly or indirectly, towards this end. Paradoxically, the fact that the welfare and happiness of individuals is inseparable from their relationship to other human beings involves an added emphasis upon the school as a community.

Summary

The book starts by focusing attention upon one small observed incident in a primary school classroom, to emphasize the importance, for a child's education, of a constructive relationship between teacher and pupil.

Technological and social changes in the twentieth century have facilitated the practical application, in schools, of ideas which formerly existed mainly in the minds and the writings of educational thinkers. Four key ideas have been examined in turn. These are:

1 respect for children and their work,
2 the idea that human beings are different from each other,

3   experience as the basis of learning, and
4   the importance of environment.

It is shown how the implementation of these ideas has resulted in such tangible developments as children's responsibility for their own learning, the exercise of choice, flexibility in the use of time and space, open-plan classrooms, group and individual work, co-operative teaching, varied resources, the extension of children's interests and more attention given to the expressive arts, to the environment and to the quality of personal relationships in the school.

The most important element in children's education is the teacher.

CHAPTER 2

THE INDIVIDUAL AND THE GROUP

To assert the primacy of the individual and to emphasize the importance of drawing as close as possible to the individual human being in understanding, when trying to educate him, is to make a philosophical and a political statement, as well as an educational one. Psychologists, concerned as they are with the diversities of human behaviour, are understandably disposed to look for individual solutions to individual problems. Jean Piaget, in his clinical researches into children's learning, while disclosing a similar sequence and pattern, discovered that concepts were grasped by each individual child in his own time according to his own level of development. Carl Jung put the individual human being in the centre 'as the measure of all things', 'the unique carrier of life', and affirmed that 'the school should be one institution above all which still takes account of the individual'.

If, in the light of present-day knowledge about learning, the concept of the individual is important in education and, more seriously, if, as Jung maintains, it is crucial, not only for education but for the whole future of society and for the world, a number of questions have to be answered before theory can be translated into practice. For the sake of simplicity these questions will be reduced to three main issues, each including a number of subsidiary ones:

1   How can individualized methods be justified?
2   How can they be applied?
3   If individuals are the centre of a teacher's concern, is there any useful purpose in studying the behaviour of groups?

These are all practical questions bearing upon the daily work and problems of a busy teacher responsible to children, parents and employers for the educational progress of a class of thirty or more individuals.

How can individualized methods be justified?

An answer to this question must also supply answers to such different questions as: are individualized methods the best for individuals? How are group needs to be met within an individualized curriculum? Are not individualized methods, involving made-to-measure resources, very expensive?

The argument for individualized approaches to teaching will be clarified when the social nature of individuals is taken into account. What characterizes a person is not only the peculiarity or uniqueness which sets him apart from others, but the human nature which links him to others who are going through similar experiences and stages of development. No individual is separate in his individuality in the sense of being completely isolated from other human beings, even if that were possible. A child from the moment of conception is already in a social situation since he owes his life to the fact of human relationship. Education for individuals is not therefore a prescription for egoism but an education aimed, through sensitive relationships and careful organization, at making the most of individual gifts and human potential. This must necessarily take human interdependence into account. The individualization of the school curriculum can therefore never mean the separation of the individual from other human beings, but rather the adjustment of learning material to the peculiar intellectual equipment of the learner, so that, within an organization which facilitates a closer relationship with the teacher, individuals who are free to develop according to their own capabilities may gain a truer insight into the needs of their fellows who are also given the same opportunities.

Are individualized methods the best for individuals?

This question assumes wrongly that an individual is in some mysterious way locked up in a hard cocoon of self, with the rest of the world shut out, and that it is to this impervious ego that individualized teaching is directed. Such methods, far from being the best, must surely hold the direst consequences not only for the individual himself but also for the rest of the community, were such methods ever to be practicable. Most children grow up with other people, communicate with others, emulate others, enjoy stories and television programmes which depend for their appeal upon empathy with other human beings, and their later schooling looks forward to their participation in a world of work with other people. How then could any teaching method be justified which excludes consideration for others and ignores not only the social nature but the human nature of children? The above question is therefore based upon a misinterpretation of individualized learning and teaching. Learning of many skills is by its very nature individual, and a good teacher will endeavour to understand and use those powers which a child can bring to his own learning; but the same teacher will also realize that there are some kinds of learning which are enhanced by being shared – stories, music, poetry, dance, art and craft, physical education and games, projects, visits to places of interest, environmental studies, as well as many aspects of mathematics and science. As long ago as 1932 Carleton Washburne maintained that certain subjects in the school needed to be individualized while others should be socialized. The emphasis today is that individualization goes on inevitably within socialization and that every opportunity is taken within the individualized work to find points of social and cognitive contact with other children in the group.

How are group needs to be met?

The teacher plays a positive role here not only in the traditional sense of making his own knowledge and experience available to children, in a digestible, interesting and timely form, but in using individual children's own knowledge and experience as a focus for discussion and dissemination within the group. Some primary schools used to have a period either at the beginning or end of a morning, known as Children's News, handled in a bright, sympathetic, conversational manner by a teacher to encourage shy children to contribute to the group, as one means of helping them to win acceptance from the group, and also as an opportunity to develop language skills and courtesies within the group as a whole, including narration, reporting, the asking of questions and, in young children, the difficult art of listening to each other. The teacher, too, not only listened, but asked questions and invariably extended the interest aroused by the individual child's comments. This mixture of individualization, socialization and teaching, common practice in many infant schools, does not need separate

periods on a timetable, labelled 'News', or 'Children's Time', like the
defunct period which used to be set aside for 'Activities', as if children were
inactive at other times, but should be the rhythm of learning throughout the
day, with the balance changing in the direction of individuals or groups or
adult guidance, according to the needs of the pupils and the nature of the
experience.

'Group needs', if they exist at all, are an abstraction from the accumulated
characteristics of individuals, seen as an average. Translated into the prac-
ticalities of education, each different teacher, anxious about class teaching,
would interpret this abstraction in his own individual way, according to
how he perceived the group. This would involve the unreal task of appeal-
ing to average intellectual ability in deciding upon aims and objectives, an
assumption, where interests are concerned, that it would be safest to adopt
conventional views about boys and girls and about the old and the young.
The group, in its turn, would react to the teacher's expectations, both in
terms of intellectual output and breadth of interests. Where there is no
room for the unpredictable, only the predictable outcome is to be expected.

A wealth of research findings has, in fact, been gathered in recent years,
showing how children respond to teachers' expectations both positive and
negative (Downey 1977).

In an individually oriented working day, the teacher associates himself
with the new intellectual strivings and burgeoning skills of individual
children, yet, as the possessor of knowledge and experience, never loses
sight of his responsibility for the forward movement and social cohesion,
warmth and happiness of the group. His day is spent talking to individual
children, encouraging them, challenging them, urging them on, praising
them and where necessary checking them, and at the same time talking to
the group, offering them choices and alternatives, providing resources and
materials, stimulating questions, inviting comments, setting up signposts
to learning, and at all times seeking opportunities for sharing, for appreciation of each other's work and achievements and for mutual constructive
criticism.

Working in an individualized way does not absolve the teacher from
being a student of child development. Knowledge of how other children of
similar age groups behave, both in this country and in other parts of the
world, can be both a useful touchstone and a reassurance, but this knowledge must be carried lightly. More useful to his role is the application of the
methods of child study to his own pupils and particular circumstances. A

brief running diary of noteworthy happenings in the classroom, of children's behaviour, their interests and conversation, will prove to be more rewarding in terms of lively work than the most meticulous pre-arranged scheme full of flow-charts and diagrams. Yet this diary, too, like the observations of others, has to take second place when a new group of pupils appears on the scene, the message being that if individuals are different from each other, then any group, because it embraces a wide range of individual personalities, will differ from other groups and teachers' responses cannot be entirely identical and repeatable. Adaptability and flexibility are key words in a modern teacher's vocabulary.

Are not individualized methods, involving made-to-measure resources, expensive?

What are these made-to-measure resources? Some of the most costly resources are those for communal use, the sophisticated technological aids, necessary though these may be, the audio-visual equipment (adaptable also for use by individual learners in the form of such devices as teaching machines, language masters, language laboratories, and tape-recorders), the film projectors, television receivers, video-tapes and overhead projectors. So costliness today in financial terms enters into both collective and individualized teaching, but in the latter case the expenditure is attitudinal rather than financial, and relates directly to a teacher's professionalism, time, patience, ingenuity, the care and thought entailed in contriving home-made apparatus, often from the cheapest materials, devising a variety of approaches to suit varying needs, observing children, making notes, as well as fulfilling the traditional role of educator, enabling children to realize their human potential. Yes, individualized measures are expensive, especially in terms of time and human effort, but they are rewarding. When it comes to catering for the idiosyncrasies of the wayward individual learner, the costly and complicated educational kit aimed at the average pupil is a clumsy amateur compared with the insight and understanding of the teacher.

How can individualized methods be applied in practice?

How can teaching methods be individualized, respect for individual persons be shown, adjustments to their intellectual and emotional differences and to their social and cultural backgrounds be made and extensions of their personal experience be achieved, when the majority of teachers in state schools are first introduced to their pupils, not as individuals, but in a group? Secondly, if all the learning is done by the pupil, what is the role of the teacher? Thirdly, does individualized teaching for thirty pupils involve thirty different lessons and work schemes?

The individual within the group

A teacher has to consider the idiosyncratic nature of an individual child and yet at the same time achieve for each child a fulfilment at a wider social and human level, a programme which includes both diversity for individuals and sharing common purposes with others. Children respond to their experiences of life as individuals, but their responses are conditioned by time and place. The length of time they have been able to gather experiences is a condition shared by others of the same age group, so not only the accumulation of diverse experiences but the matching of shared experiences is of interest to a teacher whose task is the dual one of educating individuals and building nurtitive communities. In a good primary school there is evidence of independent work based upon choice, other independent work circumscribed by the child's ability or attainment and shared work based upon social and cultural values, as well as upon common interests. A beginning must be made somewhere, and this can only be in the teacher's initial relationship to the group as a whole, establishing the framework and environment for learning before any knowledge and understanding of individual children can be achieved.

Nearness with respect

It may be objected that teaching based upon nearness to children, involving as it does no less planning and arranging of materials and environment on the part of the teacher, is as artificial as Rousseau's contrived situations for Émile, whereby the boy was trapped into finding things out for himself, under pain of being severely punished by natural consequences if he failed to do so. The approach might also be accused of being hypocritical, even the child's apparent spontaneity being the creation of the adult, and patronizing, since no child ever wants the teacher to be an equal but prefers even the most friendly authority figure to preserve a dignified distance.

There is much misunderstanding here. In the first place, though the scene is set for learning, it is based upon close and sympathetic observation and understanding of children who are not tricked into learning so much as being won over as willing partners who want to share with the teacher and with other children in tasks which call for challenge and co-operation. None of this is explicit to the children of course, but they find themselves part of a community and want to continue in it and to contribute to it. Secondly, nearness to the child does not automatically require a teacher to abdicate from the role of leader and guide and pretend to be a child again. It means nearness in understanding, watchfulness of intellectual development, sympathy with the child's peculiar problems and sensitivity in offering and withholding guidance, as a result of intelligent observation, reading, and the experience of what Froebel called living with children. Only a fully qualified adult could fulfil this role.

How near is it possible and advisable to get for the purpose of helping a child to learn and inspiring him to work? The nearest part of the universe, in terms of physical distance, is, of course, his own mind and body, his present preoccupations, interests, fears and anxieties. Much absorbing scientific work can be done using the child's own body as a starting point: shapes of faces, colour of eyes and hair, weight and height, with small displays of the earliest photographs taken of individual children to illustrate developmental changes (as well as to keep the other children guessing). Physical education could make an obvious link with mathematics and science in investigating children's differing body measurements and skills. Interests in family and home, including family pets, followed closely by the world of friends, neighbourhood and school (not forgetting the family of different creatures kept by the school: chickens, ducks, doves, goats, tortoises, hamsters, guinea pigs and jerbils, to name only a few) provide another rich area of study. Television will already have given children some acquaintance with a wider world beyond that of their own immediate experience, and these impressions need to be constantly discussed and sometimes edited and corrected by a wise adult, who nevertheless acknowledges both the power and the value of the visual image.

The ideas of distance and proximity are useful ones when working with children, but must be applied with caution and commonsense, not forgetting that geographical and historical remoteness may sometimes be nearer to juniors in terms of interest than a study of their own neighbourhood, contrary as this may seem to current theory and even to some of the suggestions made in this book. In a modern primary school the dilemma presents itself of a teacher's being accused either of imposing supposedly 'child-centred' work on children on the one hand, or of burdening them with too much responsibility for their own learning on the other. The pitfall consists in a too slavish adherence to dogma in a disregard of the pragmatism that is learned through daily encounters with children, both as individuals and as that sometimes surprising and unpredictable chemical mixture known as the group.

Making a start

For a young teacher a start has to be made somewhere. On the first day of term the acquaintance has to be made between one nervous adult and thirty excited children. The art of teaching is surely put to its greatest test here. Given that the young novice has had the good sense as well as the opportunity to explore the neighbourhood of the school and to become acquainted with its traditions (for even the most relaxed and trendy school has traditions), the delicate task of getting to know those thirty individuals has begun, and all the combined qualities of friendliness with dignity, gentleness with firmness and consistency, humour with purposefulness, variety and resourcefulness begin to make almost impossible demands.

Work has to start and the giving of free choices to a large group of strangers would probably invite disaster, so our young teacher, having nevertheless set up his room with a collection of natural and man-made objects and provided a thought-and-activity-provoking environment, giving a general impression of caring and meaning business, might well be advised to start at one of the earlier stages in the evolution of primary education: the stage of initiating the children in a group exercise of his own careful choosing, with choices rather more narrowly circumscribed than he would want once individual interests and abilities have become known. He might begin with creative work in art and craft, or the making of attractive folders for later work, during which time he can be moving round the room observing and getting to know children in conversation. Alternatively, he could introduce the children to the beginning stages of sequential work in an area of mathematics unfamiliar to the whole class but easily followed by the least able children, yet leading on to more challenging thinking, for example, the beginnings of spatial work or geometry or a very general topic which allows for freedom of individual interpretation and expression. It might be wise to settle for a theme which could eventually branch out into a great variety of matter and manner, embracing many interests and skills, areas of knowledge and topics for discussion.

The untried teacher unused to the experience of free work can still hold to the discipline of producing one manageable piece of class output, perhaps a study of different kinds of people and life-styles, involving choices of writing, painting and model-making, all children taking turns to participate in drama and cooking. Children's special interests in cowboys, footballers, ballet dancers, babies, grandparents, aunts and uncles, fictitious characters of literature or television, the nightmare figures of giants and witches or the mysterious worlds of fairies and angels would be free to range over many varied territories. Later, with more detailed knowledge of the children, choices of study and activity could be extended and more opportunity be given to extract maximum educational value from individual children's interests.

As days then weeks go by work has been done, certain goals, however limited, have been reached, and all the while relationships have been built up and a new little community with its own expectations, unique experiences, proud achievements and private jokes will have been created, held together by the pervading yet inconspicuous presence of an encouraging teacher. It is in this climate of rewarded endeavour and shared enjoyment that opportunities arise for moving towards a greater degree of individualized and self-directed work, with an extension of the range of choice. There is no blueprint to be followed, and the number of different schemes for this kind of co-operative work is as great as the number of teachers who attempt it. The first essential requirement is the firm belief that it is the best possible approach for the children in question. Without this confidence on the part of the teacher any such scheme is doomed to failure.

As the class develops into a community and individual children begin to emerge as personalities, an overwhelming number of starting points for new work will occur to the teacher as a direct result of observing the children, listening to their talk, extending the work already in progress, discussing everyday experiences of individuals or the combined experiences of the group after a visit, examining collections of objects brought to school, reviewing a book or a television programme or interviewing a visitor to the classroom. Many opportunities for talk and diversified work arise, not this time in the form of a uniform class project, painstakingly planned and tidied up by the teacher, but as a kaleidoscope of self-chosen tasks pursued by individuals or shared in small groups. On the firm basis of a well-organized class who know the expectations of their teacher and are provided with an ample range of resources in the shape of tools, books, space and opportunities to use them, the teacher can concentrate on the all-important task of education: attending to the personal and intellectual development of children on a more individualized plane.

A proper respect for theory

Peter's teacher, referred to in the introduction, may not have been consciously applying textbook psychology in her personal attention to his work, but the fact that he even momentarily became more acceptable to himself was a necessary starting point in his education.

When education is founded upon some established position without a firm basis in sound theory, as if there were some special virtue in being seen to be 'progressive' or 'traditional', there are bound to be distortions and hypocrisies. The purposes and interests of children take no account of dogma. Children are what they are. The good teacher ministers to the needs as they are observed.

'Come along Elizabeth,' said the young teacher to the restless and unemployed seven-year-old, during a free choice period. 'Find something to do, something you're interested in.' Elizabeth pouted, 'I'm so *bored* doing the things I'm interested in!' Later she said, 'Can't we have a story?' Here at that moment lay her real interest. It is all too easy to follow our own adult interpretation of what children's interests are supposed to be. This episode illustrates the annoying habit which children have of confounding educational doctrines, especially those which are too tidy but which to adult minds are logical and consistent. Children are supposed to like finding everything out for themselves, to resent being told, to be everlastingly eager to be doing and not wanting to listen. This is one truth in many circumstances, but there are other truths in other circumstances. A teacher may religiously abstain from giving information in the interests of the children's finding everything out for themselves, yet on a visit to the local baker's shop to see how bread is made, he has no objection to their listening to the baker telling them about his trade. A person studying the piano learns much by looking carefully at the music score, but would be grateful to a teacher who said, 'Try placing your hands in this way' – a skill which he could not have discovered for himself by simply looking at the printed page.

Much has been written recently on the advantages of discovery learning over straightforward teaching or instruction. Claims have been made that children are better motivated by curiosity, that they understand more of what they discover for themselves and that long-term retention is superior.

However it must be remembered that curiosity, especially in young children, is easily satisfied, often only partially and sometimes by incorrect information. The kind of motivation needed for cumulative school learning and a thorough understanding needs to be sustained over a long period of time by an experienced teacher (Dearden 1968, Richards 1973). Learning by discovery, if there is no guidance, can be completely unstructured and just as confusing as failure to understand when a teacher is imparting knowledge or information. In fact, as Ausubel (1969) reminds us, clear explanations from a teacher, with examples and illustrations and couched in the sort of language children can understand, is superior to undirected finding out for oneself. It is salutary to remember that in practice there are few real dichotomies in education, as some of the debates over theoretical issues would have us believe.

If all the learning is done by the pupil, what is the role of the teacher?

A close acquaintance with children on a practical level will in fact disclose many truths about the nature of learning. In the world of children there are no false antitheses, no contradictions in having a teacher as a central figure in the classroom who nevertheless allows freedom for personal discovery, who teaches and also lets you explore, who tells a story and includes listening among the educational repertoire of worthwhile activities, who considers that language as communication involves both receiving and giving, speaking and being spoken to on a personal level.

Misinterpretations of theory, as indicated above, have got some teachers into false and hypocritical positions. They feel it is somehow wrong to teach and that they have to behave as spectators of learning when they are really producers and stage managers. If children are learning in a free atmosphere of individual investigation and expressive activity, the teacher has created that atmosphere. If there is a warm climate of personal relationships the teacher has created or contributed to the climate. If situations are open-ended and flexible and allow full rein to a child's curiosity and creativity, it is the teacher who has arranged that it should be so. Before the children arrive in school the teacher has been there, planning and providing. The classroom already has a sense of purpose before the children have burst in upon it with their own purposes which the teacher will be careful to use. There must be aims in education, even of the most general kind, for perversely the most libertarian of educators might say that the over-riding aim is to have no aims, or at any rate no specific objectives.

The aims of primary education in the present century have been inspired by the recognition of the great potential of children of primary school age and of the conditions which allow this to be realized to its maximum. Observing the vitality and restless curiosity of most children during these years, teachers in primary schools tend to think in terms of activities, of things for children to *do*, of physical encounters with concrete objects and happenings as the necessary first steps towards abstract thinking and reasoning and a rational, balanced view of the universe and of their place in it. Bruner (1960) stresses the importance of learning by engaging in activities: children can learn history or geography by doing, that is, employing techniques of research and observation available to them, just as a researcher does at a more sophisticated level. Children come to understand their world by representing it to themselves first of all through what he calls the enactive mode.

The teacher is therefore seen as an instigator of learning activity rather than simply as an instructor. For who else is to do the learning but the learner? In a school where the individual person is the reality, the raison d'être of teachers, buildings, resources, and administration, the element of coercion is lacking. The emphasis is upon relationships, upon provision and encouragement, upon the transmission of knowledge and skill through the tapping of sources of strength within the individual, the building of confidence in these strengths, the expansion of interests and the creation of new ones. The environment, too, as well as the people in it, speaks of concern for the minds, the eyes, ears and feelings of children.

Teachers whose experience has been in a more formal situation, who are unaccustomed to open-learning contexts, will certainly have to adopt new roles which they at first may find disconcerting, and certainly more demanding, but, as we have already seen, children do not rush out to discover for themselves if there is no teacher to guide, structure and evaluate their activities and discoveries (Friedlander 1965). According to Friedlander the autonomy of the learner does not mean the devaluation of the teacher. On the contrary, his role assumes greater significance when he ceases to be 'an information dispenser' and can channel his energies into the appropriate 'uniquely personal' guidance based upon understanding of the pupils' needs. Richards (1973), following Friedlander's second thoughts with his third thoughts in order to find 'the most effective use of discovery methods', rejects the idea of any one formula to fit all examples of learning and teaching. He emphasizes the importance of consolidating as well as eliciting new insights. In this enterprise 'the wise intervention of the teacher's judgement' is indispensable.

Does individualized teaching for thirty pupils involve thirty different lessons?

It depends upon what is meant by a lesson. A child who touches a hot stove and suffers burns as a result has learned a 'lesson'. In this sense a class of thirty children reacting in their own different ways to the same experience are receiving thirty different lessons. What distinguishes an old-fashioned didactic performance, with every point laboriously hammered home, from an individualized approach is, in the former case, the fear of the diversity with which even the same experience can be received, interpreted and expressed. Awareness of this diversity makes room for many different kinds of learning: for multiple choices on the part of the learners (the thirty different lessons or work schemes already referred to), for projects undertaken by small groups or for the varied ways in which individuals can respond to the same experience whether it be a visit, a story, a play, a film or a mathematical problem. Modern education does not outlaw a method because it happens occasionally to be directed to a group or even to a whole class. What it does campaign against is the idea that there is any virtue in a teacher's striving after unanimity of response on the part of pupils. This distrust of uniformity has repercussions for the idea of comparability, for orders of merit among individual learners and for the whole concept of examinations (Burgess and Adams 1980). The assessment of performance is the latest attempt on the part of the administration to achieve a measure of accountability for what goes on in schools, in a concerted official effort to raise standards.

Schools are built, organized and administered on the assumption of human homogeneity rather than human diversity. Children are placed in classes with materials, furniture and books thought to be appropriate to their age and stage of development; so how important for the education of the individual and for the individualizing of teaching is the teacher's knowledge of group behaviour?

Can the study of groups be justified in an individualized programme?

When the most recent plea in education is for attention to the needs of the individual, is there still today any justification for the observation of a whole age group, in this case the middle years, and for the study of their characteristics, if these can be identified? How important for the education of the individual and for an individual approach to teaching is the teacher's knowledge of group behaviour? Such knowledge gleaned from books and from psychological research focused upon the behaviour of other children can only be an approximation to knowledge of his own pupils, but as an approximation it has its uses. As long as he is forewarned, it is helpful to know that certain reactions and responses, though not inevitably in the realm of actuality, are at least in the area of probability. With these reservations, the study of a group can assist the study of an individual, if only to illustrate the unexpectedness of his behaviour, to make him more interesting and to arouse the teacher to question his own assumptions. A study of child development is best conceived as a background against which the teacher builds his own observations in the action-packed arena of the classroom. In any case a beginning must be made somewhere and initially this can only be in the teacher's relationship to the group as a whole, establishing the organizational framework and the emotional climate for learning and creating a purposeful environment for work, before any knowledge and understanding of individual children can be achieved. So the young teacher's first task is to establish a positive relationship with the group through his awareness of probable responses. He could make inspired guesses about what his pupils' behaviour, abilities and aptitudes might be, or he could study child development more systematically.

The danger of deducing general laws in education from particular cases
Whether studies of children are cross-sectional or longitudinal, whether horizontal across vast numbers of a whole age group or of the same group of human beings observed in their development throughout a long period, it is hazardous to assume that the resultant picture is anything but provisional, temporary and localized, at the mercy of environmental circumstances and social change. 'The child as he is' will always escape the painstaking researches of the adult; his behaviour will vary according to whether he was born in France or Russia, in the 1960s or the 1980s. The only general rule which can be followed without hesitation is that which reiterates the priority of considering individual differences in any study of childhood. Observation of the wide variety of patterns of reaction to a given stimulus provided

by the environment forces one to see how suspect generalizations are, to re-examine some of the current assumptions about children and to realize that to be scientific means to be specific.

A line has to be drawn between general statements which may offer enlightenment, but may also mislead, and bare facts which, because they relate to specific cases, are of purely academic interest. This question is important as it raises the whole problem of the value of child study. Close observation of peculiarities in children, surely no less than the close observation of insects or of any other natural phenomenon, is of importance, even if it appears, at first glance, to be of purely academic value with no obvious practical application. A study of birds as individuals (Howard 1952) illustrates the interest of a naturalist in individual variations even in the case of species where instinct leads to more predictable patterns of behaviour than with human beings. In a psychological inquiry knowledge itself is of fundamental importance, yet the ways in which knowledge finds expression in action cannot be measured or foreseen. As the report on the Primary School suggested, as long ago as 1931, it is important for teachers both to know what children are unable to give towards their own education and to provide them with the opportunities to give what they can. A knowledge of children, even though not consciously and directly applied in educational practice, might modify teachers' attitudes to their work at least indirectly.

In emphasizing the importance of attending to the individuality of children, I merely wish to stress the need for caution in generalizing, but a reconciliation can be effected between the general statement and the bald, specific fact. Children are individuals but they are not completely different from other children. They share a common humanity and do exhibit similarities in behaviour in their reactions to their environment.

It is in this double consideration of a child as an individual whose behaviour resembles that of other members of his own subculture that the value of child study consists. It has a practical value, too, for parents and for educational, medical and legal authorities who need facts on which to base programmes of policy and action. Observations of children are to be interpreted by students not as norms of conduct but as a harvesting of behaviour patterns to provide points of departure for comparison with the findings of previous studies. In this way it might be possible to isolate some of the more enduring characteristics of childhood from those more vulnerable to change, and to examine the possible causes of such changes.

The next chapter will look more closely at ways of studying children in general and attempt to examine the characteristics of the middle years of childhood in particular.

Summary

The argument for an individual approach to teaching is advanced in this chapter. Attention is given to the justification and the application of individualized methods, as well as to the social nature of human beings.

Such a programme involves observation of children's educational development, an understanding of their intellectual problems and the ability to give appropriate help.

The teacher caters for a variety of individual and social needs by providing independent work based on choice, independent work dictated by the child's ability and shared work inspired by social values and common interests. In addition to individual projects and group work, a whole class may give a variety of interpretations of a communal experience such as a journey, a film or a story.

It is again emphasized that the success of this approach depends upon the teacher's understanding of his pupils and upon his ability to make appropriate provision for their needs. A grasp of educational theory is no less important than practical classroom skills.

CHAPTER 3

UNDERSTANDING CHILDREN

Friedrich Froebel in *The Education of Man* pleaded: 'Come, let us live with our children.' What kind of children?

In learning to teach, as in all apprenticeships, one makes many mistakes. The most usual of these are traceable to the average young adult's unfamiliarity with the thinking levels of children and a consequent awkwardness in conversation with them:

'Is scimitar a noun or a verb?' was a question put to a mixed-ability class of nine-year-olds during an otherwise enjoyable reading of *Treasure Island*. 'No, it's a kind of sword,' came the down-to-earth answer.

Another dialogue with a different class of nine-year-old boys in an inner-London school shows a greater closeness to the everyday traffic of living than to the world of abstractions; the following question was part of an attempt to teach the past tense:

'How many of you have got a kite?'

No answer.

'Well, let us imagine that you have borrowed a kite from a friend, and you say to yourself, "I *have* a kite." Then let us suppose that you lose the kite. What do you say then?'

'Sorry,' was one boy's response.

It was clear that none of these children had learned the strategies for working out what kind of answer the teacher wanted, but were answering spontaneously and no doubt either puzzling or exasperating the teacher. Holt (1964) suggests that many children fail to learn, not because they are unable to, but because the kinds of question posed by teachers are not meaningful to them. Instead of being encouraged to think about what the teacher is asking, they are instead prompted to guess at the kind of answer they think he wants.

In the nineteenth century when such questioning of young children was the rule rather than the exception, the ignorant victims would have been punished for their ignorance. Today, thanks to research into human development and the nature of children's thinking, we are able to say that it is the teacher who, in asking such questions, is guilty of ignorance in the sense of lack of understanding of children's ways of thinking. The priority of the learner's experience over externally delivered instruction, the interiorization or the internal structuring of learning and the dependence of teaching upon the learner's own mental operations were given scientific support by Piaget (1950, 1953).

In a series of minutely observed investigations of children's responses in the fields of logic, language, number, space, movement, speed, judgement, reasoning, causality, time and morality, to mention only a few of his researches, Piaget concluded that there were a number of necessary stages through which a child's thinking evolved. The ages at which children passed through these stages varied, but the sequence was always the same. There were also substages to each main period of cognitive development.

The first main period is that of sensori-motor intelligence, reaching from birth until the child begins to use language, roughly the first eighteen months to two years. This is a period when the child's mental constructions or schemata derive from his actions. Actions at this stage are the necessary preliminaries to the development of thought. He learns about his world directly through the senses, by touching, tasting, smelling and so on. This is followed by the preconceptual substage when the child's thinking, conse-quent upon his own experiences, still reflects his own egocentric viewpoint. He cannot yet classify objects successfully into permanent categories and has difficulty in grasping relationships. He is therefore not yet able to think conceptually. In the intuitive stage the child's thinking is dominated by his perceptions. He will claim that because a jar is tall and thin it must contain more liquid than one that is wide and shallow. Judgements based on such private experiences do not have the 'reversible' quality possessed by logical thought: one and two are three, therefore two and one are three, three minus two leaves one, three minus one leaves two.

The second main stage continues until approximately the age of eleven or twelve and is called the period of concrete operations when the external world of objects and actions becomes part of the child's 'inner' mental world. At this stage the child is less egocentric in his thinking and begins to be able to apprehend the world from other people's points of view, but is still restricted to finding out by trial and error. Action is still present in the child's imagination if not always in physical reality.

The third main period, approximately between twelve and fifteen years, marks the beginning of the development of formal operations or the mastery of abstract modes of thought.

Each stage is not only a development from the previous stage but is an essential preparation for the next stage. None of these can be achieved without the previous levels of thinking having been attained and in that order.

Piaget established the study of children's thinking on a scientific basis, but as he himself would readily concede in such a rapidly expanding field of research as that of human development, he has not had the last word. Some of his findings, though not his essential contribution, have been challenged by more recent research, and in particular his view of the young child's egocentrism. For example, Hughes (1975) claims that even three-year-old children are capable of seeing other people's points of view if problems are put to them in ways which involve their feelings and motivations and make sense to them. A clear statement of the continuing debate on this question is given by Margaret Donaldson (1978) who nevertheless acknowledges the great debt which educators owe to the pioneering work of Piaget for the light which he has shed upon the understanding of children's minds. Teachers in their daily encounters with children have the dual task of intellectually knowing about children and also of trying to know them as people. This is why teacher education gives prominence to readings in psychological and educational research and studies of child development on the one hand, and school practice on the other.

Doing the right things in a classroom without knowing why, in other words, without a sound theoretical basis, may have suited the rare intuitive teacher with exceptional gifts, but in today's complex and changing social conditions, students of education need to know the reasons governing successful practice.

On the other side of the same coin cognitive understanding of children is one kind of understanding and must take its place in the preparation of teachers for their work in the classroom, but it is no substitute for living with or sympathetic understanding of children. It means putting oneself in the place of the child, understanding his small stature yet his vast hopes and imaginings, considering the scale of things compared to the size of his body. It means travelling back in time and feeling again what it was like to be a young creature on this planet, wise with the wisdom of the young before the shades of Wordsworth's prison house begin to close, discovering the world again through sensation, the feel of wet sand underneath bare feet, the smell of crushed grass, the distant view of earth from a treetop or a scaffolding, total absorption of mind and heart in the act of creation or in a story, two of the greatest and most necessary motivators which a teacher has at his disposal.

Many different kinds of reading, in addition to research studies, can also shed light on the lives of children and bridge the gap between academic knowledge and sympathetic understanding. Students of education should not overlook the insights that can be gained from novels and biographies as well as the findings of sociologists.

The teacher has to have the sensitivity of the artist to understand children. Studies of child development are necessarily clinical and objective. Living with children deepens and humanizes this knowledge and throws light on the importance of observing children within a closer relationship, listening to them and asking them questions with a real wish to hear their answers. This shows a greater respect for children than the old-style interrogatory approach which required a child to guess what was going on in the teacher's mind.

The middle years

The middle years of childhood, as such, are the least documented of all the young age groups, those about which least research has been undertaken. There are reasons for this. Not everyone is agreed about where exactly the middle years lie. Are they seven to eleven? eight to twelve? nine to thirteen? What are they the middle of?

Anyone interested in learning and development is usually concerned about the foundations or origins. These are important and critical years. It is not surprising then that the study of child development is at its most fully informative for the earliest years, before the varied influences of different environments have had a chance to exert their combined and complex pressures. Another large body of research has focused upon the effects of education and particularly upon the period when problems are at their most daunting: the years of adolescence. So one reason for the relative scarcity of research into the middle years has been their comparative uneventfulness, not to say happiness, when placed alongside the measles, mumps and chickenpox of the first years and the spots, pimples and sexual traumas of the later years. Another reason is that physically, mentally, emotionally and socially the middle years are so undefined as to spread themselves downwards towards the infants and upwards towards the adolescents. No wonder that the experts on the Plowden Committee had difficulty in trying to decide where the middle was. They came down in favour of eight to twelve, not so much on psychological grounds as on educational and administrative grounds. Whereas the influence of semi-specialist teachers chiefly concerned with older pupils might be reflected in more demanding work being given to nine- and ten-year-olds, it was considered a distinct advantage that the primary tradition of individual and group work be retained for a longer period than at present. They voted against a two-year extension up to thirteen on the grounds that the middle school might thereby forget that it was still a primary school. They therefore recommended that with the age raised to twelve many junior teachers would need to deepen and extend their knowledge, while former secondary teachers would have to absorb the best of primary school attitudes and practice.

Dividing the human race on the basis of age is a relatively new practice and a western one. In the Middle Ages the young entered the adult world of work as soon as they were physically able. The same custom holds good in some primitive cultures today. In the nineteenth century child development could not be a popular subject of study at a time when human beings were hustled out of their childhood either by the demands of adult life or by the threat of an early grave.

During these present days of prolonged childhood, division into age groups has become more necessary since the state took over more of the responsibilities which formerly belonged to the family, and large-scale institutionalized care insists upon differentiating people into categories, if only for the sake of tidiness. The divisions have been based upon what have been considered to be the needs of children at different stages of their physical, social and intellectual growth. Educational needs, real or unreal, can be assumed to be the grounds upon which the differentiation into types of school, school buildings and school work has been based. So we have categories of children according to their ages, and appropriate provision based upon observed general characteristics of the age group: preschool ages and what are considered in general to be the characteristics which debar a child from school and formal education, nursery school ages and nursery schools, nursery school provision, nursery school teaching, nursery school activities, all based upon what are taken to be nursery age characteristics and needs; infant or first school ages, provision, teaching and activities leading to the assumption that there are certain characteristics of children which have dictated this provision. Similarly for the junior and middle schools with their supposedly characteristic and easily identifiable child populations, and likewise for the secondary and high schools.

Yet how easily identifiable are the middle years? Now that we have, since 1967, superimposed upon the seven-to-eleven junior age group the eight-to-twelve and nine-to-thirteen middle school age groups, are we to assume that the characteristics of children have changed and along with them their educational needs? Sociologists and anthropologists have been saying that human characteristics are so much the product of social factors that what we are observing is a change in society that has brought about changes in behaviour, and these have affected teachers' expectations of pupils' behaviour. It remains to be seen whether the sophisticated nine-year-old of today would feel happier at the prospect of rubbing shoulders in the same school with children three or four years older. On the other hand would not the potential 'top class' eleven-year-old junior feel demoted? The lengthy discussions which the Plowden Committee had on the most appropriate age range for middle school children, and the disagreements that existed among the experts, illustrate only too well the imprecise, misleading nature of chronological age as a determinant of educational need. When all the combined forces of heredity and environment are taken into account it becomes obvious that there is no such creature as the typical seven-year-old or the typical ten-year-old. According to present-day knowledge, education based strictly upon age is an anachronism. The best education today is one attuned to experience, and this takes into account family relationships and the influences received from the environment. Education according to chronological age is administratively convenient and pupils may feel happier learning with others of their own age group, but the circumstances of their lives and their own inner dispositions will produce a great variety of response in their readiness or unreadiness for different kinds of learning, and will necessitate a consequently greater flexibility in teaching. Is there not, therefore, with an individual approach, a contradiction in talking about the middle years as if they were a homogeneous group capable of being educated in the same way, at the same pace and with equal success? It is obvious that, with schools as they are, a compromise is necessary between the individualization of teaching on the one hand and provision for the age group on the other. Three facts need to be borne in mind.

First of all, a teacher today must be aware of his pupils as individuals and try to teach them as such. Secondly, certain patterns of behaviour recur as part of human development and are common at different stages of growth though the rate of maturation varies. Thirdly, in the middle school and the junior school we are concerned with a population of children for whom, as a group, the state has arranged special provision based on the assumed characteristics of the majority, and this is the majority (containing many minorities and individualities) which some teachers have presumably chosen to teach because they are noticeably different from first school and secondary school pupils.

Of the various methods of studying the developing individual – naturalistic observations, clinical procedures, experimental techniques and statistical methods – the first is the one which for practical purposes will be referred to here as being the most easily accessible and applicable to the busy teacher in the classroom.

Clinical procedures, as the term suggests, imply teams of highly qualified specialists, purpose-built accommodation and especially designed resources. Experimental techniques involve the long-term employment of selected experimental groups to compare with control groups. Statistical methods demand full-time, highly qualified mathematicians. One approach to child study can be cross-sectional which, like the investigations of Gesell, observes the behaviour of large groups according to specific criteria (Gesell 1946). This has the disadvantage of obliterating individual differences in the interests of a panoramic picture across age group or sex or some other criterion. Parents can therefore sometimes fail to recognize their children and teachers their pupils, and may worry if they do not conform to the general pattern. Another approach is the longitudinal, which, like the National Child Development Study (Cohort 1958), a multidisciplinary study of children born in 1958, and the current Oracle Study (Galton M. et al. 1980), a detailed analysis of the processes of teaching and learning based on systematic observation of 58 primary school classrooms, looks at human development and activity over a considerable length of time. This approach too has its own obvious disadvantage related to the prolonged time-scale. Sampling has to be undertaken very carefully. With the lapse of so many years the introduction of new inventions, technical improvements, changes in teams of workers and in their organization may lead to mistakes. There is also psycho-analysis which is obviously outside the professional scope of the teacher. However, in the primary school realm of the nonspecialist, observations of children do go on nonstop even in the act of teaching. An appreciation of the uniqueness of an individual can be grasped when seen against the backcloth of the expected characteristics of his group. If, for example, a ten-year-old child's behaviour is unexpected, what is it that was expected?

In looking at the middle years many investigators have dealt with the period in passing while really concerned with some specific aspect of development; for example, studies of children's art, the growth of language, the development of interests, children's ideas of religion, cognitive development including various studies of learning viewed from the outside, as in the work of Skinner and the behaviourists, and learning experienced on the inside, as in the clinical researches of Piaget or the probings of depth psychology.

Children in the middle years are, in general, involved in Piaget's stage of concrete operations and barely entering upon the stage of formal operations and abstract thinking. They are also involved in what Freud calls the latency period, after the passage of infancy up to the onset of puberty, known in its simplest terms as childhood, according to Freud a period of calm and stability before the disturbances of adolescence. They are years of consolidation. If one thinks in simplistic terms and in an overgeneralized way of various phases of human life as being characterized by the existence of certain over-riding psychological needs, it is possible to identify the vulnerable and helpless years of infancy as being dominated by the need for love and security. With this secure base established, the active and questing behaviour of the young junior appears to indicate a need for finding out, for adventure and experiment, expressing also a need for mastery, for achievement and acceptance by one's peers. Conformity to the mores, fashions and language of the peer group assumes great importance in adolescence, while the young adult seeks above all to achieve a measure of self-acceptance and a sense of personal identity and significance. This oversimplified ladder of human growth may help, in a diagrammatic way, to locate the middle years as a time of physical and mental mobility and intellectual curiosity.

In common with human beings of all ages, children like to be accepted as they are. They are eager to be originators and for their interests to be taken seriously. Teachers sometimes make the mistake of thinking that a child is wanting approval, when all he is longing for is for someone to acknowledge his existence, to encourage in him a feeling of confidence and personal significance. This can be done even without saying very much, and without the cursory comment of praise or approval, but simply by participating in a child's interests and by showing some general enthusiasm and animation over his current preoccupations. Teachers are so used to giving marks and assessments, to offering opinions, as from one who knows, that they wrongly imagine that children need approval when what they require is recognition and acceptance, and for some interest to be shown. This objective is sometimes sought in ways little calculated to win approbation! As with human development in general, child development can turn sour and suffer from distortions under adverse environmental pressure or deprivation. Ill-adjusted children can be most badly behaved towards those whom they love the most, and whose love they most desire, as a means of testing that love, and the natural urge to experiment and explore can turn to vandalism and destruction, especially in the company of a peer-group gang from whom the child wants acceptance. Parents who have maintained communication, and regularly talk about everything under the sun with their children, have an obvious advantage even over those experts who spend most of their professional lives instructing, judging, approving and disapproving.

Summary

Effective teaching depends upon a teacher's understanding of those who are to be taught. Though this book emphasizes the importance of adapting education to individual differences, the present chapter seeks to justify the need to study those characteristics which a group shares in common, the group in this case being children in the middle years. A knowledge of the age group is important for a teacher who, as well as trying to teach children as individuals, must be aware of those individuals' identification with their own contemporaries, and aware too of recurring patterns of human behaviour. The teacher also has responsibility for the welfare, education and progress of a specified group for whom appropriate provision has been made. It is also assumed that, for reasons known to himself, the teacher has chosen to teach this particular age group rather than another.

CHAPTER 4

SOME CHARACTERISTICS OF CHILDREN IN THE MIDDLE YEARS

Some characteristics of children in the middle years form a background against which the differences which distinguish individuals need to be seen. Taking only 'normal' healthy children as examples, the following tendencies of the age group seven to thirteen years, including junior and middle school children, appear to harmonize with the traditional purposes of teachers. They are:

1 The desire for achievement, responsibility and independence.
2 The desire to learn and to explore.
3 Activity of mind, body and imagination.
4 Acquisitiveness.

There are inevitably other, less applauded forms of behaviour and these deserve study if only to set teachers on the track of looking for more 'acceptable' alternative interests for their pupils.

The desire for achievement

This characteristic is not peculiar to this particular age group or to the educationally gifted. Indeed McClelland (1953) claimed that a need for achievement was a basic motivating factor in all of us. Workers with very young children and babies strenuously affirm from their observations the repeated efforts of infants to gain mastery over their environment. Dr. Maria Montessori, in a lecture delivered in London in 1946, talked of the child's need to engage in 'maximum effort' to conquer the environment, and of the importance, for both physical and psychic development, of providing for him opportunities to carry heavy objects and to practise difficult movements. Older children and those in their middle years often draw attention to their ability in feats of daring. It is possible that in these self-imposed tests of skill and courage a child depends for his self-esteem as much upon being acceptable to himself, according to his own standards, as upon the good opinion of others. Emulation of other enterprising children seems to be one way in which a child proves his potentialities to himself as well as to onlookers. Thus J. McV. Hunt (1971) refers to complexity or competence models who may be adults, or older or more skilful children, whose behaviour spurs on those less competent to match them in skills and achievements. During playtime at one school, one feat of daring was seen to lead to others of progressively increasing difficulty. The short-lived publicity surrounding the skateboard industry undoubtedly depended for its effectiveness upon this characteristic of the young learner. Observation of children during many playtimes showed that the harder the feat was, the greater its attraction. Children were often to be seen performing strenuous and difficult feats alone. This suggests that satisfaction in the accomplishment of a hard task does not necessarily wait upon the presence and the approval of others. At other times children did demand a spectator to witness their prowess ('Sir, watch me!'). To judge by what children themselves say, the finest reward is work itself, with achievement as the most conspicuous incentive:

'Sir, do you like my Norman castle?'
'What do you think of my story, miss?'
'I've just made up a poem, miss. Would you like to hear it?'
'Sir! I've knocked all my nails in straight first time!'

Among the lessons which listeners to these remarks can learn are, firstly, the importance of providing freedom, time, space and materials for achievement in worthwhile tasks of the children's own choice, and, secondly, the importance of the sympathetic ear as children talk about their work. We note too the importance of an immediate appreciation of the child's effort and commitment to his task, and the great value of a thoughtful, carefully considered evaluation of the child's product. (This is where we came in with Peter and his important fish.)

The inappropriateness of marks, prizes and team points is obvious. The reward for having built a bridge is having built a bridge, an event which actually occurred when part of a playground was deeply flooded by torrential February rains and the children took upon themselves the task of constructing a perfectly efficient, dry footbridge across the newly formed lake.

Sometimes children in their play impose the most strenuous exertions upon themselves in obedience to a fantasy. On a sweltering hot day in June a group of four nine- to ten-year-old boys at an East London play centre were seen toiling up a steep, grassy slope, carrying a heavy tin trunk full of 'treasure' on the way to their camp in the bushes. The treasure consisted of bricks, paving stones and large lumps of concrete. The power of imagination was a more potent influence upon their behaviour than bodily fatigue.

To the obvious satisfaction of teachers many children normally wish to excel in schoolwork as well as in their own favourite out-of-school pursuits. The wise teacher tries to arrange a marriage between the two, and there is no question of sugaring a pill if the attractiveness of difficulty is fully appreciated. Alongside the many examples of children whom I observed in junior and middle schools, seeking the status of people who could be trusted with more responsibility rather than less, acting host to visitors, answering the headteacher's telephone, helping with tree-felling, wheeling the coke-trolley for the elderly caretaker, scrubbing out a paint cupboard, vying with each other for the job of cleaning the blackboard, demanding to be a leader in school projects, there were instances where, in academic studies too, children were anxious to shrug off their childhood and reach out for more advanced work. In my own teaching experience this was particularly applicable to mathematics, especially when a new topic was approached and children felt they were making progress. They asked for more and for harder sums. One cannot ignore, even in a formal approach, the sheer aesthetic satisfaction children can get from achieving a neat page of sums.

If one considers, too, the aesthetic aspects of another basic skill, handwriting is best taught as art rather than as exclusively tied to formal English. In the case of the children referred to earlier, once the skill of writing had been mastered and enjoyed and children were free to write at their own pace from their own experience, they again asked to do more, eventually making their own books and requesting to continue writing them at home.

In their reading, which tends to increase in quantity as they grow older through these middle years, the declining interest in fairy tales and magic which held their attention in the earlier years, together with their occasional disparaging remarks about 'kids' books' and 'girls' books' (a dislike sometimes shown by the girls themselves), may be further evidence of the striving to outgrow childish things, the desire to grow up and live the 'hard' life beyond the world of childhood. It is significant that the favourite book of the children in question was *The Children of the New Forest* about children for whom responsibility for adult tasks was the order of the day.

It must also be said that in these middle years, for all their strivings towards adulthood, children are still children, and a certain polarity of behaviour may be observed in which the essential dependence of childhood is discernible beneath all the brave attempts to achieve some small measure of independence. Together with examples of behaviour which appear to suggest that a child is reaching out towards adulthood and finds satisfaction in being 'stretched' in this direction, a teacher working with this age group will come across examples of behaviour which, in some cases, seems not merely typical of childhood, but, where certain individuals are concerned, seems surprisingly childish, as though the effort to hold their own as competitors with older people were sometimes too much for them, and that the pastimes of children might provide a safe retreat. The teacher who is aware that the general trend of healthy development in these years is towards maturity need not therefore be alarmed that certain children who appear to be unusually domineering and independent in one type of situation can be noticeably insecure and dependent at other times. During adolescence also, feelings of self-assurance, personal adequacy and independence from adult authority are still goals to be aimed at rather than reached.

The desire for achievement, so noticeable during the middle years in the child's physical exertions and often too in schoolwork (of a suitable kind), is a dynamic which finds overt expression in shameless pride, boasting and extensive use of the first person singular in conversation. At the upper end of the age group the blatant boasting of the younger junior gradually and subtly gives way to the self-consciousness and greater social sensitivity of the young adolescent. This is illustrated in the following conversation in which the prevailing accent is on pride, pride in achievement, pride in personal experience and pride in possessions, of which the child's family is one. The talk, during school dinnertime, was initially about aeroplanes, between a group of juniors aged between nine and ten, in which the airing of knowledge about aeroplanes appeared to be of greater importance than listening and receiving knowledge.

Jack: 'I went to the aircraft museum. I've been in a Rolls Royce Merlin and seen a 6000-horsepower one.'
Tony: 'Daddy worked on the airfield.'
Patrick: 'I have been on the fastest train in the world. It goes to Leeds.'
Susan: 'My sister went in a canoe down the river with a friend, all the way from Hammersmith to Waterloo to see the lights.'
George: 'I have been through all the Thames tunnels.'
Ian: 'They started building a Channel tunnel.'
Patrick: 'I know all my Tenderfoot knots and can tie them in the dark.'
John: 'I passed a lot of cotton mills in the holidays. I saw the cotton being taken to the mills and unloaded. I went fishing and caught two trout.'
Tim: 'Has anyone ever been to Lagos by British Airways?'
Jack: 'No.'
Tim: (after a pause) 'I have.'

This is hardly a conversation as adults would understand the word, though one cannot deny that even very young children are capable of carrying on a continuous conversation (Tough 1973, 1977, C. and H. Rosen 1973) but psychological factors, for example, the desire to be acceptable to one's peers, rather than linguistic immaturity, can affect the character of a child's communication with his fellows. With the exception of Ian's follow-up of George's talk of tunnels, the only common factor in the above exchange is the personal pronoun 'I' or the possessive adjective 'my', as if the speaker were using the occasion to win recognition for himself or his family. It tells us something of the child's journey on the road from social immaturity to maturity. Again a polarity is noticeable between dominance on the one hand and dependence on the other, a desire to achieve significance, an urge to contribute, against a background of reliance upon the goodwill of others, strength having a struggle to emerge out of weakness, though the weakness is unacknowledged. So wrapped in egocentricity is each child during the talk, that he is determined to impress the others, although, paradoxically, knowing that all have the same intention and remain unimpressed by each other. The direction of the talk may well have been influenced by the presence of an adult and by the children's striving for acceptance, observable on other occasions. To what extent the competitiveness of contemporary society contributes to this feature of child development is beyond the scope of this book to explore, but teachers can verify for themselves that the striving of children to outgrow childish things, along with the ambivalent tendency to rely on adults for support, is a conspicuous characteristic of the middle years. Children at the beginning of this age group are in a transitional stage between egocentricity and social awareness, and at the older extreme they can still be described as socially immature, the boys more so than the girls. Yet the urge to grow up is strong. The desire to achieve, so conspicuous in games and physical pursuits, is not lacking in other directions as well, shown in many ways, intellectual, manipulative and linguistic. The cry for excellence in education, so often uttered in the daily press, on radio and television, is never more intimately, though secretly, echoed than by children themselves.

The desire to learn

Considering the amount of energy expended by a healthy, growing junior, not only when challenged by his physical environment but also when teased by intellectual problems, there is in his mind ample demand for exertions and excursions, for enterprises and inquiries during his working day. Along with his desire for achievement, and closely related to this and to his striving for acceptance by his contemporaries, is the child's need to learn, not only to learn about but to learn how. Mind and body are close allies in the same crusade for knowledge and skill. Just as his thoughts and plans and fantasies find expression in physical ways (toiling up the hill in the heat with his 'treasure' of concrete blocks), so the child's body, as in the case of the infant, is still a nonverbal instrument for intellectual inquiry. With his body, as well as with his mind, he asks questions, not only about himself and his capabilities, but also about the nature of the world as he finds it:

'Will this branch bear the weight of my body?'
'How deep is the water in this pond?'
'Where does this tunnel lead to?'
'What will a spider do if I put something in its web?'
'What sort of noise does a fence make when you run a stick along it?'

This kind of behaviour is also on the side of the educator, one of whose most important functions is not to get children to give the right answers so much as to get them to ask the right questions, 'right' in the sense that they lead to further thinking. On the other side of the coin children also explore the human environment and find excitement in provoking reactions from adults:

'What will they do if I knock at the door and run away?'
'What will happen if I tap my ruler in class?'

A child's desire to learn can sometimes cut across a teacher's desire to teach because the world of childhood is not a world of school and classrooms and rows of desks (rarely seen now anyway in primary schools), but it is nonetheless a world of learning, of curious inquiry into the meanings of things, into repeated experiments in bodily and mental skills. Yet it does not exclude the world of adults, for many of the answers to children's questions and their achievements in the realm of physical and mental skills are gained from imitation and from appeals for guidance and support, however indirect and disguised these appeals may be. This is the role for which teachers are fitted. Children today are fortunate in having the sophis-ticated resources of film and television to answer many if not all of their questions. The greatest danger which these media of mass communication hold for the education of children is that they do their job too well, before the children have had time to ask their own questions, and therefore rob them of the essential experience of exploring and finding out for them-selves. The teacher has a duty here not only as a watchdog to keep television at bay until the time is ripe, but to provide the experience and stimulate the questions. With television in almost every child's home it must be acknow-ledged that it would be extremely difficult for the teacher to be first on the scene. It is nevertheless important, with so much second-hand experience available, that efforts are redoubled to supply as much first-hand experience as possible, and this is generally done today by means of visits, school journeys, collections of natural objects in the classroom, museum corners with loans from local museums and art galleries, art and craft work, physical education and movement, making musical instruments and outdoor activities such as gardening, keeping animals, setting up a bird table or a weather station, mapping the neighbourhood and environmental studies which involve local people.

The traditional role of the teacher was that of the sage who knew it all, giving the world to the child from his vast store of knowledge in the form of lessons in the sciences and the humanities, as if all this knowledge were somehow to be injected exclusively from outside. Teachers today, it is hoped, know better. They are well aware that the child's mind is not a *tabula rasa*, but that he is both a part and an inheritor of the world. The teacher is dealing with a being whose starting point for learning is in a knowable environment. Not only does the present-day teacher take account of the fact that the child is in the world, but also that he carries his own world within him and it is this world which modern education, after nearly a century of research, is seeking to understand.

Teaching methods try to keep pace with the findings of child psychology. For example, the emphasis in junior and middle schools on such activities as environmental studies, neighbourhood projects, archaeology, natural sciences and excursions relates to the fact that, in contrast to the egocentric preschool child and the introverted, self-absorbed adolescent, the child in the middle years tends to look outwards. Generalizations like this, of course, are too simplistic and can be misleading. They can never absolve the teacher from the all-important and absorbing task of trying to understand the individual child.

Activity of mind, body and imagination

If we happen to watch a group of primary school children who are free from the supervision of adults, perhaps the fact which impresses us most about them is that the things which they choose to do involve so much that is overtly physical. We have seen that even a fantasy which is mental in its origin finds expression at this age through the larger muscles of the body. On approaching a primary school playground we most often hear the children before we see them. One hears much unrestrained noise, loud laughter, screams and squeals, shouting and talking in shrill, high-pitched voices. The child's energy is so dynamic that it embraces every part of his body, including voice and lung power. His energy is global. No wonder that the opening chapters of so many autobiographies clothe the childhood of the writer in an aura of wonder and nostalgia, a kind of hymn to health, now seemingly at its best. Voice does not yet appear to be differentiated from the child's other powers. Just as he puts his whole energy into throwing a ball, so his whole frame seems to vibrate with the throwing of his voice. A well-modulated voice adjusted to the size of the room and to the ears of the listener is something the younger junior has not yet achieved, so when he speaks he tends to shout. As we come nearer we see children running, jumping, climbing, skipping, hopping, walking the tightrope along a wall, balancing, swinging, dropping from heights, turning somersaults. One requires an incredible number of verbs to describe these children. It is wise therefore for a teacher of this age group to think of learning provision in terms of activities and to associate their learning with things to *do*. Given good health the child in the middle years is seen to broaden the physical investigations of his environment with which he began his life. Whether out of school or in school, or in spite of school, the quest goes on. New objects have to be touched, and strange places like caves or puddles or empty houses have to be explored. Trees and scaffoldings have to be climbed. And with all this adventuring an inner conversation is going on in the mind which is the voice of imagination. This is no builder's scaffolding but the elevator tower of a rocket. This is not a bicycle but a racing car. I am not sitting in the sand pit. I am crossing the Channel in a boat. I am not coming downstairs to breakfast. I am Cinderella making my entrance down the grand staircase at the ball, and this is not an old lace curtain but the most beautiful dress in the world. According to Piaget, the experience of action, in the physical sense of active encounters with the environment, would appear to be important for the growth of thought. Successful mastery of the environment is both a motivator and a reinforcer of learning. Mother says, 'Why don't you walk properly?' but John doesn't want to walk properly along the pavement but along the top of the wall, or upside down along the branch of a tree. The sight of a middle-aged man or woman doing the same thing would give cause for disquiet. This obvious and apparently common-sense observation that the behaviour of children is different from that of adults raises the question, Why? What characterizes the behaviour of adults? The word maturity may spring to mind, but what is mature behaviour? Consider the curiosity, bravado and sense of daring associated with a child's first bicycle ride. Think too of a child's first visit to the seaside, especially by train, the sense of wonder on leaving a great city terminus through green countryside towards the unknown, and then the first sight of the seemingly limitless expanse of water. Contrast this with the tired commuter's daily return home to the coast. Is not one aspect of so-called adult behaviour the expression of a familiarity with the environment which no longer invites curiosity, a blaséness towards everyday objects, places and experiences which disappears when the annual holiday promises something more romantic or exotic? Apathy of this kind can all too soon attack the adolescent in his attitudes to the familiar world of home, school and neighbourhood. Junior and middle school children, on the other hand, being new to the world, have so much to find out about it, and to find out by means of their bodies as well as their minds. So they must investigate and experiment and get the physical feel of things. Immaturity calls out for exploration. A teacher in a primary school, without being childish, is like a child in that he vicariously enters into the delights and freshness of everyday experience alongside the children with whom he shares his daily life and work. He sheds any world-weary wisdom which he may possess and in the company of the children is as excited as they are with what, to him, are the sights and sounds of an everyday but enduringly remarkable world. In this his behaviour is neither adult nor immature, but visionary. He is gifted with double vision – an insight into the wonder of the universe with its endless possibilities for learning and discussion and creation, allied to a deep empathy with the nature of children. The French have a profound distrust of what they call *enthousiasme*, which is often used disparagingly to denote a spurious, superficial emotional gush which, like a firework, explodes into momentary brilliance and is then just as suddenly extinguished. The enthusiasm of a teacher for his work is of a different kind, and has a permanent glow when it is doubly rooted in understanding of children and curiosity about their world.

The physical behaviour of children in the middle years is indicative of a need for active movement, but it is indisputable that the great importance attached to physical education is because of its benefits for psychological as well as bodily development. We have seen that children ask questions with their bodies, even though the questions are not consciously formulated, and those responsible for providing the nation's schools seek those kinds of environment which will permit freedom of movement. Social development also keeps pace with the child's growing conquest of his world. As children become increasingly sensitive to the expectations of their fellows, so we find that a large amount of prestige and consequent self-respect becomes linked with the ability to perform innumerable physical feats. It is a cause of great pride to be able to climb the tallest tree in the spinney, to be able to swim a length of the baths, to be able to balance along the top of the monkey walk, to be able to spit the furthest and with the greatest accuracy and to be able to go cross-eyed or double-jointed. There is evidence, too, that children in this age group admire feats of endurance or daring in others, as well as trying to attract attention to their own physical achievements. In their reading and television viewing they enjoy stories of adventure in which the laurels go to the bravest. In stories of crime and mystery, success must come through a combination of brawn and brain. In most of the schools where I was able to make observations, knowledge of professional football and cricket, as well as of the finer points of some individual performances in these games, was valued by boys and often aired at playtimes and mealtimes. Power, strength and speed were often referred to in their conversations and admiration for these qualities extended likewise from human beings to machines. A knowledge of the latest machines, particularly aeroplanes and those which moved at high speeds, was generally considered by both girls and boys to be valuable mental equipment for a modern child. The appeal of trains, ships and cars was also evident from their discussions which often involved showing off their familiarity with technical details. When Jackie innocently admitted that she did not know the name of an aircraft which had just flown over the school, expressions of scornful surprise came from her classmates, both girls and boys. They exclaimed, 'Don't you know that's a Vampire Jet? Fancy not knowing that!' The craze for speed and the modern child's interest in aeroplanes, rockets, fast cars and motorcycles were a cause for anxiety on the part of a mother who gave vent to her feelings on this subject at a parents' meeting. She was worried about what she considered to be the false sense of values and particularly the distorted valuation of money and wealth which tended to result from a preoccupation with such things.

Reality and make-believe

Whether or not today's children are more materialistic than their predecessors, it is undeniable that the world of modern technology is a strong competitor for their attention and interest, though it is also noticeable that at some time during the middle of the junior school years, between the ages of eight and nine, the worlds of make-believe and objective reality exist side by side, with the former only gradually giving way to the latter. Fairies and talking animals still feature in some favourite stories of eight-year-olds; then, for many children by the age of nine, these are beginning to compete in interest with some of the everyday miracles of modern science. It must be emphasized that opportunities for developing scientific studies are ready-made among the prevailing interests of today's children, and these are being catered for even in the infant and first schools. Though children in the middle years still need nourishment for their own inner world through stories and first-hand adventures of admired heroes, there is a growing irritation with the extravagances of some writers. In a conversation about stories, a group of nine-year-old boys all agreed that they preferred stories about real things and probable happenings to stories of magic like the *Arabian Nights*. During a reading of *Emil and the Detectives* one boy showed impatience with the element of fantasy when he said, 'I hate it when people have dreams in stories. Can't we skip the dream part?' The general scorn for fairy stories shown by this particular nine-year-old class was highlighted by a girl who, in order to tease her friend, announced for all the class to hear, 'Jill is reading a fairy story', to which Jill, her face flushed in protest and self-defence, replied, 'It's not, it's a legend. So there!' There appeared to be a hint of fraud for these children in situations where the wave of a wand set everything right. Real life was not like that. They now had sufficient sense of social justice to realize that mistakes must be lived through, not easily dismissed by magic trickery. Stories in which phenomena of this kind appeared invariably met with groans and such remarks as, 'That's silly. That couldn't happen.' The child's intellectual inquiries are drawing him closer to reality as adults conceive it. 'Cor! doesn't it make you sick!' was one boy's comment on a miraculous and highly improbable escape, as a result of supernatural intervention. Yet, in a story firmly located on earth, possessing an authentic and preferably a recently studied geography, children will swallow wholesale the breathtaking adventures of other like-minded children. 'It's a smashing book,' said a boy at the end of a quiet reading session. 'It's the story of a boy inventor. He invents a rocket car balloon, a diving bell and a boat with a gun that shoots sharks. It all takes place in Australia about ten miles from Melbourne. It's jolly good.'

There is no doubt about the important place which stories do and should occupy in the lives of children. For many of the children to whom this book refers, no time or place seemed to be unsuitable as the occasion and setting for a story. Quiet periods during the lunch hour, when small groups were gathered round a table, were favourite times for listening to stories, but some children were indifferent to the inconvenience of time and place and never seemed to tire of asking for a story to be told. Some even asked for a story when being escorted to the bus stop at four o'clock. On the coach going to the summer camp children asked to be told stories above the roar of the traffic, and in spite of interesting things to be seen on the journey. There were occasions when the children themselves enjoyed telling stories, and at dinnertime took it in turns to be the story-teller, a different child each day. There was 'Rita's Nightmare', 'The Seaside Horror' and an action-packed saga about a helicopter, a submarine, a cave, flashing lights at night and a great deal of fighting in which the villains were always defeated. The climax of this story was reached when the wheels of a pursuing aircraft knocked over and killed one escaping villain, then caused a car to swerve and kill the other.

Though children in the nine-to-ten age range expressed impatience and disappointment with stories in which there was an element of magic, many of them still enjoyed make-believe in their games. Realists where stories were concerned, they nevertheless liked to play games in which they could impersonate other people or even animals, and improbable happenings were not taboo. A group of girls revelled in imaginative games of this kind. Having once established their identity as boys or men or horses, on make-believe foundations, the superstructure of the story which they then proceeded to act out claimed to belong to the world of reality. Great attention was paid to detail. In one of these games the girls had to be Scottish boys, not just boys. It was the miraculous and the magic rather than the improbable which, from about the age of nine, began to be outlawed both from reading and from play. The element of escape from the immediate everyday world of school and suburb, and identification with the bold, the brave and the beautiful, persisted throughout school life. Boys and girls who perform superhuman feats demanding both intelligence and courage beyond the powers of mere grown-ups, and by so doing save civilization from extinction, still seem to be firm favourites in children's fiction, and do not suffer the fate of Alice in Wonderland whose popularity has to wait upon the discriminating tastes of older readers. Not all grown-ups, however, fit into the pedestrian moulds of parents and teachers. Young juniors can be held spellbound by the accounts of life in earlier times told by old people, and can give serious attention to the fireman and the policeman describing their work. This responsiveness to the attitudes and feelings of other people shows a growing social awareness, and a good school has a permanently open door to visitors from the wider world outside.

Children's play in the middle years can often best be described in terms of drama. Sometimes a story told in school is continued out of school in the form of dramatic play. There was the occasion when Odysseus was seen rushing round the playground brandishing a stick and a dustbin lid in pursuit of Polyphemus. Two other boys on another day were pretending to be the elephant and the elephant driver from *The Golden Island*. These and other examples illustrate the value, for a teacher, of knowing stories which stir the imagination sufficiently to be enacted out of school hours, and they show the appeal which the dramatic element in a story makes to a child in the middle years. Sometimes a large group or even a whole class would become involved in playing out in their leisure time an experience which had moved them during school hours. Some of the children's classroom experience found spontaneous expression in vigorous bodily movement and in dramatic play.

During one playtime an entire third-year class were playing a chasing game. Those who were being chased had handkerchiefs tied across their faces, covering up their noses. When asked what the game was, a boy said, 'We're playing Black Death He. When you are caught you have to take your handkerchief off, and that means you've got the Black Death and you have to help catch the others.' When asked, 'What are those children doing standing in the corner of the playground?' he replied, 'They are in Scotland. If you can get into Scotland the plague won't reach you so you can't be caught. You are immune.' The liberating effect on children's language noticeable in this episode is also illustrated by an incident at a Southeast London play centre for children recommended by the local Deptford authority as being in special need. The children came to the centre hungry for play and for the creative experiences denied them in the dingy streets. On her first visit to the play centre, Stella, an extremely withdrawn eleven-year-old, refused to talk to anyone, bent her head at the approach of a grown-up, and when spoken to, responded only by a furtive, frightened look. Her liberation was brought about by an old evening dress, formerly the property of a member of the staff, a pair of high-heeled shoes and a length of chiffon. On subsequent evenings Stella invariably arrived at the play centre with a closely guarded parcel under her arm. It contained a pair of red, high-heeled shoes. 'They're my sister's,' she announced proudly to the onlookers. These shoes became an essential part of Stella's inspiration as an actress. Then one evening a member of staff, seeing Stella painting, asked, 'Aren't you going to dress up tonight, Stella?', to which Stella replied emphatically, 'Oh no! I haven't got my shoes.' Later observations of Stella became a history of her growing confidence and fluency while acting. One evening Stella, dressed in a long, black, ragged evening dress, high-heeled shoes and a broad-brimmed straw hat, was acting in front of a small audience of younger girls also dressed up. Stella soliloquized for at least half an hour without a break, making up plays as she went along. Sometimes the stories were fictions of her own imagination, and at other times they were dramatizations of stories which she had obviously heard at school. The many dolls and puppets from the toy box were each introduced in turn as characters in the plays. There were King John (spoken of in majestic tones), Rufus, Robin Hood, Maid Marian, and Cinderella introduced as follows: 'This is Cinderella. She is very beautiful. This is the Ugly Sister. And this is a stepsister. She's not very nice. She's me.' After that introduction she told a long story which involved taking the puppets to different corners of the room – one corner was a dungeon – where they were later joined by other puppets. As she warmed up to her story Stella's vocabulary was enriched by longer words. She appeared to be enjoying the sound of them, regardless of malapropisms. With violent gestures and an expression of great anger she shouted, '. . . and the Queen was *outrageous*.' This normally reticent and almost inarticulate child, rated as backward at school, described as 'daft' and 'crazy' by members of her family, with very little command of written English, was developing a flow of well-constructed sentences of which the following is an example: 'Maid Marian, separated from Robin Hood, began to cry . . .' This was followed by her own story of a rat and a cat, then a coherent, unhesitating account of the story of Cinderella, but for all these performances it was absolutely necessary that Stella should be wearing the red high-heeled shoes and any other dressing-up materials she could find.

Acquisitiveness

The collecting of information about people and things through all these various ways – physical exploration, questioning, play-acting – coincides with a hungry acquisitiveness and a developing sense of property. Just as the junior greedily picks up scraps of information, so he may start collecting almost any object that takes his fancy. In some cases the objects collected bear little or no relation to any useful purpose, or even to the supposed interests of children. This is acquisitiveness in its purest form – collecting for the sake of collecting. Colin made a huge collection of used firework cases and brought them to school. When he was asked what he was going to do with them he said he did not know. Some of the collections of older children do show a more utilitarian purpose. Sometimes they seem to manifest an intellectual or scientific orientation and at thirteen may reveal a more specialist interest. Many nine-year-olds like to collect and wear badges and some are beginning to make serious collections of stamps and coins. At the age of eleven Tim had an impressive collection of badges, insignia and even uniforms which were directly related to a growing interest in the armed forces, war stories and especially naval battles. Anthony collected seeds from fruits for planting in his private garden. These he kept in a matchbox in his desk.

The fondness for making lists is another possible manifestation of the collecting tendency. Tim's bedroom was lined with pictures and lists of badges, ships and weaponry. Ben spent one term compiling a list of medieval sports and pastimes. It must be admitted that throughout his middle years Ben displayed a precocious and obsessive interest in history. This expressed itself not only in the classroom but also in his play. Ben's enthusiasm was caught by other children and he was the guiding spirit behind such invented group games as Black Death He, Crown Jewels, involving two warring nations chasing each other all over the playground, the capture of prisoners, the making and waving of flags and banners, reconnaissance parties, neutral zones, spies and hostages, with rules made up as the game evolved, and a similar game necessitating elaborate preparations for War Against the Girls, following a lesson on Joan of Arc.

In a similar mood Frank spent some careful hours compiling a list of kings and queens. Graham had different interests and in his own time both in and out of school was writing down a detailed list of British birds.

Such collections and lists referred to very specific interests, some of which were short-lived. It could not, for example, be said that because Graham spent so much time talking and writing about birds, he was therefore interested in natural science. Like many other children he enjoyed many of the activities associated with creatures that moved, such as watching animals, birds, fish, reptiles and amphibia. He liked making plaster casts, pond-dipping, dissecting owl pellets, constructing a bird table, going on a fungus hunt, making a map of birds' nests or birds' songs, going for a nature walk or following a nature trail. He showed no interest in sedentary studies of natural science. Trees and flowers bored him unless the work involved some physical or creative activity such as bark-rubbing or making plaster casts of leaves. In a similar way it could be said that Ben's passion for history was not so much the dedication of the adult historian (how could it be?) as a delight in all those activities associated with history, the visits to museums, making models, collecting pictures, dressing up (Ben said, 'The Middle Ages is my favourite time, I would have loved to wear armour'), acting out historical scenes in the playground, such as tournaments and the Peasants' Revolt, not to mention his many games of battle and bloodshed.

If concepts are the results of thought processes which associate objects or ideas according to some characteristics which they have in common, then, according to an experiment on concept formation in 200 primary school children aged five to eleven years reported by Brown et al. (1975), it would appear that there is a wide range of individual differences in children's ability to understand and use adult class concepts, and in young children these concepts evolve slowly. It is not surprising then that the appreciation of a category known as history or science is not fully grasped by children in their early middle years when the attractions of learning consist mostly in the opportunities it offers for active energy, new experience and personal achievement. Towards the end of the middle years there is a general trend towards the use of sophisticated class concepts as age increases. A teacher might then expect a greater understanding from pupils of the significance of subjects in addition to the enjoyment of certain activities associated with them.

Knowing children as individuals and as members of groups

The aspects of children's behaviour selected for comment are simply some of those of which an observant teacher might make practical use. They are 'positive' rather than 'negative' or destructive tendencies (though many acts of destruction may indirectly serve a constructive purpose or feeling), and, for teachers who have spent a lifetime observing children, they are the more enduring characteristics of childhood, applicable to children today as to children twenty or thirty years ago. Children have changed in many ways in the decades since the end of the Second World War, in their attitudes to authority, in their choice of heroes, in their apparent sophistication and knowingness, in their familiarity with modern technology and in their earlier maturing. The world too has changed and with it the hidden education which children receive from their surroundings. It is a world of urban expansion, of changes in society and changes in the home. There are greater state and community responsibilities for welfare, changes arising from modern inventions and from labour-saving devices which release mothers from domestic toil into the world of employment. Added to these are the means of travel and communication which extend the frontiers of knowledge. Inevitably, too, have come changes in social attitudes affecting ideals of equality, human rights, including those within marriage, women's and children's rights and the rights of minorities in a pluralist society. The last half of the twentieth century has seen changes in attitudes towards morality, marriage and sexuality, and differences in the treatment of one-parent families. There are greater resources for leisure, existing paradoxically alongside environmental conditions dangerous to children and hostile to children's play. Yet at deeper, more universally human levels, like characters in classical literature, children differ remarkably little from young human beings of earlier times. They still exhibit, sometimes all too transparently, the need for love and security. Most of them are eager for adventure and novelty and for exploring the unknown. Children in times past and present, whether in physical skills, kicking or throwing a ball, carving a boat out of a piece of wood or in the mental exercise of solving a puzzle or breaking a secret code (reading is like this for some), offer a picture of creatures anxious to achieve mastery. To gain acceptance from one's admired fellows, either from genuine achievement or from notoriety, has always been and still is one step towards self-acceptance. Personal identity is a journey, not a destination, and at every stage certain needs emerge into prominence. Children of eight to twelve, having been set on the journey towards identity by love, protection and security in their earliest years, as members of a family circle with rights to their own ways of thinking and feeling and aware of the rights of others, are particularly remarkable for their curiosity, their need to learn, to explore, to discover and find out for themselves, to achieve and to win acceptance from their fellows, a characteristic which comes to greater prominence in adolescence. Personal identity, given the satisfaction of these needs, goes on growing throughout adulthood. For a teacher who wishes to know pupils as individuals it is useful to know them as recognizable, or in some cases unrecognizable, members of a group.

Children's apparent tendencies to behave in this way or that are never so generalized as to be completely predictable. The individual case is always a factor which complicates the general picture. While this already widely accepted knowledge is uncomfortable for the kind of teacher who likes tidily laid schemes of work planned on formal class lines, it is welcomed by those teachers, no less conscientious, who prefer flexibility and adaptability to the peculiar gifts, interests and problems of individual pupils. Generalizations themselves when met at classroom level have to be adjusted to suit individual needs. If, for example, one considers the general statement in the report on the Primary School (Hadow 1931), 'that the curriculum is to be thought of in terms of activity and experience rather than of knowledge to be acquired and facts to be stored', the teacher is still left to find out what kind of activity is needed by the individual child and when. During my observations as a teacher I noticed that at certain moments in a child's day he appeared to enjoy stillness as much as physical activity, and some children seemed to need these periods of quiet absorption more than others. The nature of activity itself, when considered in relation to the teacher's knowledge and understanding of the individual, comes to be thought of in more than bodily terms. Children in their moments of quiet, mental concentration were highly active. A teacher, therefore, choosing work for children according to the 'active' principle, would be misguided in avoiding certain intellectual pursuits just because they happened to be sedentary. So many years have now elapsed since the publication of the pioneering 1931 Hadow Report that sensible practice today acknowledges the broad interpretation of activity in a just balance of physical, intellectual and imaginative skills which was then recommended though sometimes misunderstood.

I became aware, too, that some children's activities were transparent expressions of emotional need, so no general prescription taken from an overall study of child development could be applied in the absence of knowledge of the individual and his motivation. To take one example, Linda, singled out for special schooling, belonged to a category vulnerable to all the hazards of stereotyping: the backward child. At her first school her slowness in the basic academic skills of reading and mathematics made her conspicuous among her more able classmates. Yet she was unquestionably a unique individual with peculiar gifts and talents, most noticeable in the direction of domestic skills: needlework, knitting, housework and general usefulness to others. She wanted, above all, to be liked, to be appreciated, and for her contribution, whatever it might be, to be valued. She desired praise for her services far more than she desired gifts and services from others, except where these were clear expressions of love and liking for her. She was warm and open, talkative and spontaneous to those who showed her warmth, but estranged, frozen, inhibited and tongue-tied with those who graciously tolerated and patronized her. She spent a great deal of money on presents and repeatedly wanted the assurance that these had given pleasure. She liked to be thanked and longed to be noticed. She constantly needed the expressed confirmation that her services and achievements, however slight by normal standards, were recognized. Once when she was part of a group engaged in a conversation which was above her head, she suddenly disappeared then reappeared with ice-creams which she had bought for everyone, as if to say, 'I can't join in your clever conversation but at least I can buy you all an ice-cream'. Linda was anxious to learn and wanted to read. Teaching her to read was achieved mostly by making use of her desire to communicate. She was encouraged to write letters, and from this beginning she slowly improved in both writing and reading. She now writes letters without help, no longer needing to copy the prepared statements of somebody else.

In my earlier years as a teacher I found that, even within the apparently unemotional area of learning activities, thinking only in general terms about children and their supposed needs did not always bring success. On one memorable occasion, acknowledging the importance of constructive activity for children, I gave a girl something to make, but the 'something to make' was conceived only in general terms as a good recipe for education related to an age group, yet unrelated to the child's peculiar personality. She did not want to make anything in the given context and asserted that she was not good at making things. On the other hand, when liberated from the classroom, many of the activities she chose formed a constellation round her particular obsession of the moment: horses. With her little group of friends she busied herself building a stable with odd pieces of wood they had carefully collected. At other times she was discovered sitting alone in a corner of the playground making a bridle out of paper clips linked together or reading *Black Beauty* or drawing horses. Obsessive yes, but also constructive.

Children can be allies of teachers when the teacher's knowledge of child development relates more closely to the individual. The makers of school timetables are at pains to bring balance and unity into a child's day with a judicious proportion of constructive occupations, intellectual accomplishments, including language and mathematics, reading and manual skills, physical education involving both the functional and expressive abilities and imaginative activities. However well balanced this diet appears to an observer, the unity of the picture is ultimately provided by the child himself. In the last example quoted above, though there was an outward change of activity, from building, to manipulating paper clips, to reading, to drawing, the inward mental activity was still faithfully pursued. It is this inner activity which has to be probed if children are to be understood.

Summary

Following the recommendation to study groups as well as individuals, even within an individualized work programme, Chapter 4 singles out those characteristics of junior and middle school children which conspire to make them eager learners and allies of the observant and understanding teacher. Along with most other human beings, they desire to be accepted as persons in their own right, but four characteristics have been selected as being particularly helpful in the school setting. They are:

1   the desire for achievement,
2   the desire to learn,
3   activity of mind, body and imagination, and
4   acquisitiveness.

It is hoped that the examples given of teacher action in harmony with these observed characteristics will be taken as descriptive rather than prescriptive. Caution must be exercised against the temptation to generalize when studying the behaviour of a group and to apply a recipe for education which ignores individual differences. However enlightening the study of groups may be, the predicament and progress of the individual learner, with his peculiar abilities, interests and talents, are still the teacher's main concern.

CHAPTER 5

THE ENCOURAGING SCHOOL

Education in social values

As research has shown, certain concepts, for example, ideas of space, number, the world, morality (Piaget 1950, Kohlberg 1966), are grasped by individuals in their own peculiar way and in their own time. These findings, occurring as they did in a social and political climate sensitive to the expression of individual rights and freedoms, served to reinforce the educational trend towards individualizing the curriculum, and much valuable ground was gained in this direction. Important battles have been won for children, especially those in primary schools, as a result not only of the growing interest in children as individual members of the human race, but also of increased knowledge of the personal and peculiar ways in which they learn. These are firmly established landmarks in the history of education and it must be emphasized that a concern for children as individuals in no way contradicts the importance of their social nature as members of groups. Schools which are known for their sensitive treatment of children and adults as individuals, in other words, for their respect for persons, are usually also famous as warm, social communities. In catering for individual interests and propensities the careful teacher is always on the look-out for opportunities to encourage sharing, whether it be sharing experiences, ideas, work or material resources. Ironically, a class taught as an undifferentiated mass with an eye on competitive attainments comes together in groups with group concerns in mind less easily than one in which individual differences are democratically fostered and developed. Too many victories have been gained by primary schools on the psychological and social as well as on the

organizational front for the education of children as individuals for the
process now to be put into reverse, though vigilance is always needed in the
face of public anxiety and political pressure. Inertia and reaction have a
dynamic of their own to inhibit progress, however well documented. This
call for alertness on the part of 'progressive' teachers was undeniably
applicable to education in the 1970s when, following the call by the Prime
Minister of the day for a 'Great Debate', as a result of worries in governmental circles about one school in particular, and also about educational standards in general, there has been a noticeable swing away from concern with
the interests of the individual child towards more nationally oriented preoccupations. This movement has assumed various forms, including a call for a
common core curriculum and pressure towards a revision of the public examinations system, though it must be conceded that proposals for a reorganiza-
tion of school government, allowing for more participation by parents and
the local community in addition to the responsibilities and freedoms formerly given to headteachers, their staff and the local education authority
should not, given a supportive membership, threaten the welfare of pupils.

Such developments should not, however, affect the essential purpose of
education which, after so many struggles and so many advances, still
remains not only the education of the unique individual towards the realiza-
tion of his own peculiar potentialities, but also the contribution of freely
functioning individual personalities towards the building of a positive,
caring society.

These aims are not irreconcilable, though recent research (Ashton et al.
1975) into the aims of primary education has shown that teachers tend to
attribute greater priority to one of the two: some consider the aim of
education to be a preparation for life in a given society, while others place
greater emphasis on the value of independence and individuality. Perhaps
those who constructed the questionnaire should not have worded it in such a
way that these two aims were automatically assumed to be mutually incom-
patible. A proper care for the individual child must surely involve helping
him to develop socially.

Schools have not traditionally been slow to establish their own peculiar
codes of social behaviour, but adherence to a venerable tradition must not
be confused with social education in a more general human context. A
situation in which children are expected to conform to an accustomed social
pattern highlights the nonconformity of those who are unable, for physical
or intellectual reasons, or unwilling through emotional or temperamental

reasons, to match the behaviour of others. Standards and norms are the enemies of eccentricities and differences. If social norms are to be the guide, whose norms are to be followed? Where children are encouraged in their individual differences and interests, unpredictable strengths are tapped and the teacher's life is full of surprises. Not enough is expected of children in terms of output or personal quality. Their potentialities are greater than those envisaged by the most demanding of teachers. A teacher's plan for a whole class may actually impose a restriction upon the aspirations and capabilities of certain children. A social climate in which differences are not only tolerated but welcomed is not one to encourage the growth of stereotypes. It is true, however, that children in groups, when left to themselves, often tend to exhibit stereotyped, insensitive behaviour towards a nonconforming or exceptional individual. For example, Sally, the tomboy, was always a target for teasing, while Tom was another butt, a prey to childish jokes because of his large size and slowness of movement. It may not be thought that there is anything particularly alarming or harmful in such behaviour. But an element of sadness is present in the reactions of the two victims. Children are separate, independent individuals; it is this uniqueness that a sensitive teacher strives to protect and develop. Children are also members of communities, and as social beings they react to social situations. Teachers are controllers if not creators of such situations.

Both Sally and Tom reacted to their situations in the spirit of 'If you can't beat them, join them'. Sally began to see herself as the great disrupter of other people's play, the tomboy who deliberately provoked boys to chase and rag her. She started her life at the school by being good-humoured under provocation and quick to retaliate. This behaviour encouraged other children, who rose to the challenge. She enjoyed boisterous horseplay, the excitement of the chase and eventually being sat upon beneath a great pile of bodies. A later more disturbing development was her initiating the teasing and tormenting of younger children, snatching away their toys and interfering with their play. Tom's being overweight became a group problem in that the group developed certain expectations in the light of Tom's size. He was developing a whole set of personality characteristics oriented to the expectations and jibes, however affectionate, of his companions. In response to their predictable behaviour he began to over-react, exaggerating the slow, ponderous movements of the heavyweight, speaking breathlessly and laughing at his own attempts to master certain physical skills. He could, of course, have over-reacted in an opposite way by striving to become more agile and lightfooted than his slimmer and more athletic friends.

It is natural for children to react spontaneously to the differences in others, whether they be differences in physical contours or idiosyncrasies of character; but unanimity of reaction and monotonous conformity of behaviour, when uninfluenced and unguided by rationality and compassion, can amount to unkindness, even to persecution and to suppression of undetected human potentialities. Who could have guessed that Sally, the teased and the teaser, both bullied and bully, was an accomplished dancer? Or that Tom, slow-moving and 'hopeless' at games, was brilliant at art? It is in social education quite as much as in academic attainments that teachers come into their own as professionals. If human beings are prone from an early age to fall into the lazy habit of stereotyping their fellows, then the social climate needed to counteract this tendency has to be created. In an accepting social climate, young children are quick to accept others along with their differences. The conventional labelling of individuals in the everyday world of adults is in marked contrast to the unconcern with which children at a present-day play centre for juniors choose their various activities, some of the boys choosing to knit while girls do woodwork. Modern primary schools no longer segregate the sexes for craftwork and cooking on the basis of traditional male and female occupations. Boys enjoy domestic activities as well as carpentry, and girls have a similar breadth of choice. When Stephen joined the Scouts and went to camp, he became much in demand as a champion cook, showing different character traits and abilities that had previously been unsuspected at school, a forcible argument for including cooking for boys as well as girls in a rich and varied school curriculum. Children need to be put into groups small enough to allow them to talk to each other, listen to each other, share activities and understand each other. This is particularly relevant in a multicultural classroom. Situations must be created in which people can work together and share their problems and achievements. The adult should help the group to appreciate the value of diversity and eccentricity and should arrange situations in which individual contributions by their very unpredictability are accepted and enjoyed as delightful surprises. The likely victims of teasing or unpopularity or neglect can then be seen as contributors in a variety of serious or light-hearted situations. A teacher in such circumstances would be so keen to understand the emerging personalities in the group that his main interest would be in terms of 'What do you think?', 'What is going on in your heads?', 'How do you feel about this task or this experience?', rather than 'Guess what is in my head and give me the right answer'.

Some modern primary schools, in creating caring, welcoming and accepting communities, are thereby re-creating individuals. The diversity of gifts is positively encouraged, so that no eccentricity or idiosyncrasy causes the raised eyebrow of the teacher or the jibes and teasing of the children. The curriculum caters for a wide variety of interests and allows a multitude of choices and modes of expression. In a rapidly changing, liberated society, it should not appear extraordinary for a secondary school girl to be attracted to bricklaying and a boy to be interested in embroidery; and no individuals should be allowed to suffer embarrassment because of unusual choices. The lives of many famous poets, musicians, dancers, painters and saints are so often overshadowed by the struggles outstanding geniuses have had against the mockery of their contemporaries and the disapproval, alas, of their teachers.

Experience is individual, but it can also be shared. What could be more educative and healing than the sharing of ideas between a wise, understanding, questing adult and a curious, inquiring child? Education can be stereotyped according to sex, and it can also be stereotyped according to age. When education is geared to experience, however, both age and sex become irrelevant. The excited observations and comments of a nine-year-old boy, on his first flight with his parents to America via the North Pole, were as acceptable as those of the adults. Within a shared experience, it becomes difficult to say at a given moment who is the teacher and who the taught. A good school fosters this kind of verbal exchange from a wealth of first-hand experiences. Each person can extract from them and bring to them his or her own unique offerings. In so doing they discover themselves as well as each other. The effects of experience are unpredictable – a source of endless surprises and therefore a delight for the teacher whose enthusiasm is not dampened by knowing everything in advance. Questions become real when the answers are genuinely sought.

Many questions are asked in school by teachers who already know the answers. How insulting most adults would find such questions to be if asked within the context of a normal social gathering of adults! Stubbs (1976) criticized what he calls the pseudo-dialogue that some teachers use. Questions in class do not have to be inquisitorial. They can be inspirational. Solutions to genuine problems may take a variety of forms:

'We could cook a meal with these Elizabethan ingredients to find out what their food tasted like.'

'We could make up a play and bring in this old-fashioned song . . . and try out the dance movements.'

. . . 'Yes and we could dress up . . . where's that book on fashion? . . . perhaps we could invite our parents.'

'I'd rather make one of those concertina folders about it.'

'I want to paint a picture or do a frieze.'

'Three of us would like to make a model.'

'I want to carry on reading.'

Some schools have a flexible concept of educability across age, sex and ability groups. Teachers show their respect for persons by acceptance of diversity of interest and output. Renouncing all rigidity in their expectations, they set no limits to the potentialities of the learner. Each child is encouraged to aim for the best of which he or she is capable, within a rich variety of human activities. A key concept in the school's philosophy would be responsibility: the teacher takes responsibility for his children, including their behaviour towards each other, and for the warmth of the classroom social climate, while the children are responsible for their own learning and for sharing the efforts and fruits of co-operation with others in work and in discussion. There would be an avoidance of authoritarianism on the one hand and of sentimentality on the other.

Children are happy in a school where they can work hard with a sense of purpose, responsibility and a feeling of achievement. Slow learners, too, want their achievements to be recognized. Why else should Linda, singled out for special treatment in a large barracklike hospital for the mentally handicapped, be at such pains to exhibit her poor little achievements, her polishing and dusting, her bed-making and the stain so painstakingly removed from the bath? Later improvements in her social and intellectual development came about when she was removed from the hospital and given employment among friendly people who valued her for her specifically personal qualities.

It is good for teachers to have understanding of the general picture of child development, to be able to make appropriate choices of books for children and to have a well-documented concept of 'normality'. It is equally good to carry this general knowledge loosely; to be prepared for the unusual interest, the wayward and whimsical use of words, the eccentric and atypical child. When education is for the whole kaleidoscope of human activities, for tolerance of the unforeseen and for acclimatization to uncertainty in a world of fast-changing roles and mixed roles, stereotypes might gain little foothold. In a world where differences are valued, no one should be tormented for being different.

While the teacher is attending to one child, perhaps Peter with his fish, what is happening to the rest of the class, the thirty-four other children who are also individuals? This is the kind of problem which preoccupies present-day teachers who are caught between the modern research-based demands for a more individualized approach to teaching and the Victorian economy-based legacy of oversized classes. It is therefore timely to examine the various ways (there is no one blueprint) in which different teachers have experimented with class organization in their daily endeavours to meet the needs of individual children within a large group. An all too frequent picture has been that of the harassed teacher snatching a moment to stimulate and reinforce Peter while an ever-lengthening queue of children waits for 'spellings'. In classroom management the thoughtful teacher has had to be concerned not merely with the deceptively pedestrian questions of 'How many groups?', 'Who sits where?' and 'Who will work with whom?', but with deeper issues involving the very nature of teaching itself and the role of the teacher. These issues include the ability of primary school children to work on their own, the degree of responsibility which they can assume for their own learning, the worthwhileness, in educative terms, of certain interests and self-chosen tasks (some of which might just as profitably be pursued at home without the intervention of a teacher), the amount of guidance and direction which is required by particular children, for lack of which learning comes to a stop and boredom and discouragement set in, as well as the happiest ways in which to win children's attention and concentration upon their work, necessary for any intellectual advance, avoiding or minimizing the distractions occasioned by noise and movement too often (unfairly) associated with group work.

Teaching

Teaching is an art which is becoming increasingly dependent upon scientific method, and its essence, which is commitment, exemplifies the fundamental difference between the nature of science and that of art. The scientist is detached in his approach to the object of study. He is objective in his thinking, and the results of his work will, as Aldous Huxley (1963) has pointed out, culminate in a public statement: 'Carbon dioxide is a gaseous compound of carbon and oxygen' is one use of words related to scientific investigation. The artist, on the other hand, is attached subjectively to his idea, even though his knowledge and skill are derived from science. The statements he makes come from a world of private experience albeit uttered in public: 'Bare ruined choirs where late the sweet birds sang' is a private, and therefore unique, arrangement of words.

Teachers must know about children. They must also know children. One kind of educational knowledge is gleaned from scientific journals and from the researches of psychologists and sociologists. Another comes from personal involvement with children. Some of the most distressing mistakes in teaching come from the personal side. Children should enjoy education, but there are times when they experience only anxiety and guilt. The personal nature of the teacher's function, with an emphasis upon communication and understanding between individuals, makes the act of teaching, with all its scientific and technical supports, more closely akin to the work of the artist. Teaching as art is most relevant to the education of young children for whom the world as sensed is more appropriate than the world as described, though it is undeniable that descriptions of the world and knowledge from books are indispensable to the education of older children and adults, for whom the accumulated intellectual wealth of mankind cannot become first-hand experiences for every individual at the level of sensation.

Do the conditions for practising an art exist in the classroom? As is the case with other arts, teaching flourishes best in conditions which allow freedom to the artist to do his best work. Upon this freedom of the teacher depends the child's freedom to learn. Important though the material conditions are, the personal relationships which provide the emotional and social atmosphere of a school or classroom are at least as vital to children learning. People rather than buildings and equipment are responsible for such educational necessities as freedom for working and thinking, spontaneity, sympathy and experiment. On the negative side, too, it is people who can interrupt work, kill enthusiasm and shatter mental concentration with bells, sudden changes of period on a timetable and harsh, nagging voices. Fellow-learners, too, may be a source of disturbance. Education requires conditions in which there is time to work, time to think, time to grow, time to come to your *own* conclusions, conditions in which there is an ample supply of interesting material and challenging activity, and opportunities to learn and gain a feeling of progress.

Creativity is a word much used in referring to the arts. How does this apply to teaching? If teaching is an art it is naturally an advantage to have enjoyed practice and skill in other arts, but creativity in teaching has more to do with people than with things. Like other forms of creative activity it means bringing into being awareness, values and attitudes that didn't exist before, and if teaching is a creative activity it is, among other things, creative in fostering individual potentialities and in building positive human relationships. A group of children or students comes together at first as an administrative unit, arranged chronologically or alphabetically, but if their grouping is to be educative it should evolve as a social unit, held together by positive feelings and purposes. This is the responsibility of the teacher. It means creating harmony and co-operation where none existed before. It means building hopeful attitudes towards learning and work and other people, in the place of merely neutral or even negative feelings.

Amid the stark realities of urban crowding, large classes and increasingly limited resources, there are teachers in innercity primary schools whose days are spent replacing negatives by positives, building knowledge on the wasteland of ignorance, understanding in place of suspicion and distrust, awareness in place of insensitivity, skill in place of clumsiness, strength in place of weakness, vision in place of blindness, truth and accuracy in place of falsehood, inaccuracy and sentimentality, beauty in place of ugliness, good in place of bad. Teachers whose work has this constructive quality cannot conceal their excitement about what is to be communicated and their excitement in the act of communicating it.

Ease of communication, which is essential for a learning group, does not come about by accident. It is created by the teacher who provides the opportunity for children to be themselves and produces the conditions for frank and fruitful talking and receptive listening. Like the children, teachers, too, learn to listen. Without listening there is no communication. But education is not only dependent upon listening. It involves looking, seeing, imagining, thinking, judging, making and many other activities.

The problem of how to win children to the task of seeing, doing and thinking for themselves led educators of the twentieth century to study child nature, motivation, learning and group behaviour, and to evolve an objective and scientific approach to education. With insights gained from the now massive accumulation of findings from research in child development, psychology and sociology, teachers are convinced of the responsibility which each individual has for his own learning as well as the power which environmental influences have to enhance or to depress both intake and output. It becomes the task of the teacher to be not only the sensitive artist but, with some scientific knowledge as his support, a craftsman in creating the most favourable environment for his art.

The evolving classroom

'The best of primary education' has never meant leaving children alone, unguided and untutored. So much has happened in the school before the children enter upon the scene, for the scene has been set by the teacher, and the headteacher has preceded the staff by ensuring that the whole environment of the school speaks to children and staff alike. Flowers and shrubs may grow near the school gates, a tasteful selection of plants and fabrics, pottery and paintings can furnish the entrance hall. 'Someone has been here before us' is the message of the school and classroom environment. The children have not been first on the scene, yet there must also be accommodation for the view that the playground is made for the children and not the children for the playground. So there are trees which show signs of having been climbed, logs lying in disarray where children have tried their balancing skills and hard-beaten earth where their feet have trodden.

Finding the best way of catering for the individual child within a large class has been and must continue to be a matter for individual experiment on the part of the teacher with no blueprint to follow. As if following another kind of recapitulation theory, many young teachers in their first post have proceeded cautiously in ways similar to those traced by the history of English primary education itself.

Old-fashioned as it may sound, there are still three main ways of organizing for learning, and all are to be found, with varying emphases, in good primary schools. Children can be taught in classes or split into smaller groups or given freedom to study as individuals with guidance. As might be expected, the more recent emphasis has tended to be towards an individualized approach, though, according to the Oracle team, such methods, in the classrooms they observed, were at a managerial rather than a probing and personal level (Galton et al. 1980). Though the act of learning is something no teacher can achieve on behalf of the learner, nevertheless the learner has to be brought to this act by the skilful persuasion of a professional teacher. This can only be accomplished when relationships are such that there is mutual understanding between learner and teacher, and the latter has sufficient experience to be able to accommodate the intellectual needs of the individual within the work of the group. But what to teach when, at the beginning of a teaching career, the personal circumstances and intellectual condition of pupils are unknown? In the early stages of a teacher's experience, with over thirty children in the class, what to teach is a less difficult question to answer than how to teach it. There are certain human abilities related to social living in the civilized world upon which a child's self-respect depends: the management of his body with its accompanying skills, the ability to communicate with his fellows through language and some knowledge of his environment. The world is full enough of enjoyable visual images, shapes, colours, sizes, sounds and movements, people and creatures with their adventures in space and time, for there to be no shortage of themes and activities from which to choose, daily encounters to describe, re-create and dramatize. But how to offer these treasures so that they will make their maximum impact upon each individual child? It might be useful to consider this question in terms of distance or, preferably, nearness, in relation to the learner, so let us examine two practical aspects of the teacher's work: classroom organization and choice of learning material.

Classroom organization

To talk of the evolving classroom can make no sense without a backward glance at history, if only to appreciate the extent of the distance travelled by the practitioners of education. The evolution of the English classroom is all too often mirrored in the efforts which a present-day experimentally minded teacher makes in the attempt to escape from an old-style pattern into the modern world. Gradualness is the watchword in both cases. From the old to the new, where learners are concerned, is a progression from remoteness to nearness, and the stages, though not so tidily separate, are roughly as follows:

Stage I Rigidity

The classroom has a front and a back with fixed desks in rows. Teaching is expected to consist largely of formal pieces of instruction bestowed, at a confident pace, almost as a gift, from one person to the whole group. Where the teacher is single-minded, impatient of interruption, concerned more about the delivery of the message than its reception, the result, from a well-behaved class, might be silence and stillness, the very result he might be hoping for. Yet no teacher really believes in such apparent passivity. Underneath the silence and the immobility minds are at work, building and destroying. There is not just a single, uniform response to the teacher's stimulus, but a many-headed monster, a diverse response, as varied and complex as the individuals in the class. Variety would be the keynote in the reactions of a good, lively, interested class. Another class might be much less homogeneous, with some dissenters and some who lag behind. In the most disastrous of teaching situations the whole class might take mental flight from the teacher towards other, more attractive, more urgent interests. So even in the most formal of organizations, individuals, despite all outward appearances of conformity and subjection, will react as individuals. It is no exaggeration to say that a teacher giving a lesson to a class of thirty pupils is giving thirty different lessons. The lecture type of lesson, just described, exemplifies the idea of distance from the learner at its maximum. The obvious failure of this approach, especially where young learners are concerned, is bound to raise questions in the education system and in the minds of all inquiring teachers worried about methods which they have inherited from the past. Is a teaching situation necessarily one in which children learn? Does learning only take place within certain architectural shapes, with particular arrangements of bodies and furniture? Does it need an optimum number of participants, and if so, how many is the optimum number? On what basis is this number arrived at? Economical, administrative, psychological or educational? How many teachers and how many learners should there be in a group? Must there always be only one teacher? Must the learning group always be a class of more than twenty learners? Cannot the teachers and the learners sometimes change places and exchange roles? Is the learning only on one side, and should there be two sides? Is not a learning situation necessarily a social learning situation, and are not all the participants therefore learners? Is a lesson something that is given by one person to another? Whose lesson is it, the giver's or the receiver's?

Questions such as these prompted the evolution of the primary school classroom and its very gradual emergence from the early stage of rigidity.

Stage 2   The beginnings of mobility

The first stirrings of change in education, away from the rigidities of the earliest years of mass instruction, were due to a number of different influences, the strongest of which came from the educators of young children.

Teachers of infants have a long tradition of child study and a distinguished line of educational pioneers to guide them in their thinking, if one calls to mind the names of Friedrich Froebel, Maria Montessori, Margaret and Rachel McMillan and Susan Isaacs. It is hazardous to try to ascribe educational advance to any one set of influences, because the history of education is so complex and the forces for progress stem from so many sources, from teachers in classrooms, from conferences and courses, from books, journals and articles, from advisers, inspectors and government reports, from innumerable meetings, both formal and informal. In the education system in England and Wales particularly, where freedom has been a watchword, schools are so diverse that it is difficult, if not self-defeating, to distinguish one above all others that has set the most successful pattern for others to follow. Yet the above-mentioned pioneers associated with the education of young children have left their mark upon education in this country. They are widely separated in the circumstances of their work. In the nineteenth century, in a picturesque, wooded valley in Thuringia, Friedrich Froebel founded his kindergarten, and through the influence of his life and teaching became the inspiration of the Froebel movement, which was to spread far beyond the frontiers of Germany and encourage others to open schools where the study of children was the starting point for teachers. In a contrasting environment, in the slums of twentieth-century Rome, Maria Montessori, at her house of childhood, insisted upon the importance of adapting the educative process to the stage of mental development of the child. To this end she applied to young children some of the methods that had been successfully used for educating handicapped children, in which education by touch was of paramount importance. Before the First World War Margaret and Rachel McMillan, in deprived parts of Deptford, were working to persuade people that dirt, disease and malnutrition must be eliminated before education could succeed. Their names are most closely associated with the development of the nursery school and with work on behalf of the preschool child. In 1924 Susan Isaacs began her research on intellectual growth in young children, based on psychological records of work carried on at the Malting House School at Cambridge. These children were from professional families, and were all well above average intellectually.

These pioneers, different as they were, had at least one characteristic in common: their theoretical work, as well as their teaching, was based on close encounters with children, living with them, observing them and as teachers attending to their needs, recognizing the significance of their native capacities and the importance of freedom in their education.

The teachers of infants in England and Wales, convinced not only by the achievements of the pioneers and the growing work of the child study movement, but moved also by their own commonsense and empathy with young children, realized that the education of the very young, to be productive, could not be 'prescriptive, categorical, interfering' (to use Froebel's own unflattering description of the contemporary Prussian education), but must necessarily take its cue from observation and study of children themselves.

The infant schools were therefore the first (in more than one sense can their successors today be called first schools!) to extricate themselves from the strait-jacket of rule-book teaching, rote learning and fixed seating.

Another influence making for greater mobility in the classroom was the introduction into the curriculum of art, with all its disturbing consequences. For example, art required desks to be moved. It was also the subject where some choice was allowed. But complete choice of activity was still in the future. Children could paint this or paint that, but everybody was painting. All pupils were engaged in the same kind of activity at the same time. Desks were moveable but, except for the art lesson, were still in rows. Art, however, was the best base from which to move into the area of personal taste, discussion and sensitive relationship between teacher and child (as with Peter).

It was during the late 1920s and the 1930s that, through the work and influence of Marion Richardson, children's art was set free to become an authentic expression of the artistic impulse. Thanks to Marion Richardson, too, design and pattern began to replace drudgery in children's handwriting (Richardson 1935).

Stage 3   Choices may be made
With the recognition of the dynamic value of art in the intellectual (Eisner 1979) as well as the emotional development of children, the conditions for its proper functioning in schools produced beneficial side-effects on the whole learning scene. The area of choice began to widen, first of all within art itself, with choices not only of subject matter but also of different materials, to include clay, textiles, wood, stone (and later many varied substances), then the idea of choice spread to other subjects.

The invasion of the classroom by the revolutionary idea of choice meant not only the pursuit of different activities at the same time but the use of different resources, some of which could not be comfortably housed in the same work space. Thus in education an idea in the mind becomes a tangible object in space – a sink or a work bench, a lathe, an electric cooker or a tiled floor.

Stage 4   The break-up of class teaching

A logical development from the idea of choice was the thought that children working in the same material would best be grouped together. Admittedly it seemed best to the teacher, from the point of view of class control, because the class still existed as the main teaching unit. The social benefits for children who were thereby gaining experience of sharing tasks, ideas and resources were not fully realized until later. The work of the groups was still directed by the teacher and was still within the confines of one subject. Direction and control of groups was most in evidence where the basic skills of reading and mathematics were concerned. Developments in the organization of these basic subjects will be dealt with separately. Though some schools had just abandoned streaming by ability, work was carefully graded, children were arranged in sets and meticulous records of individual progress were kept. Indeed, the nearer a school came towards an individualized programme, the more urgent the need for such recording was felt to be. Examples of the development of work in reading and mathematics, to be given later, further illustrate the gradual liberation of teacher and child from the stranglehold of mass teaching, from enslavement by one prescribed textbook and from the lockstep of uniform progression.

Stage 5   The beginning of integrated or undifferentiated work

Familiar to infants' teachers for at least two decades as their normal way of working, without being distinguished by any peculiar label, the integrated day made its belated appearance in the junior school during the 1950s, although in many junior schools even today it is not the established practice.

It could not be long however before those teachers who had had successful and satisfying experience of allowing children to work in groups doing different things, either within the confines of a subject or a 'Project' (spelt then with a capital P and conceived initially by some teachers as a superficial marriage between geography and history and culminating in a model plus scrapbook plus wall display), made advances into the bolder adventure of broadening the work to include different areas of the curriculum simultaneously, though still holding a tight rein on the organization. This was a time in the late 1950s and early 1960s when classroom walls in nonpurpose-built nineteenth-century buildings began to be systematically demolished, windowsills were brought lower and corners or bays fabricated to accommodate work in maths and science, language, art and craft, as well as providing a quiet library corner. It required great courage on the part of the inspired pioneering headteachers who, with their old-fashioned school buildings, dared to confront teaching staff, parents and children with such a bold attempt to reproduce in the teeming heart of the innercity the more congenial working conditions and flexible environment enjoyed by schools in other parts of the country. The amount of movement involved in this freer way of working was revolutionary and frightening to some teachers who preferred something more circumscribed and controllable, so in some of the more cautious experiments a set time was given to the work of each corner and then it was 'All Change'. Groups would rotate so that so much writing and reading were balanced with so much mathematics and science, then so much art and expressive activities. The different interpretations of integrated work were as numerous as they were contradictory, yet the whole movement was exciting and forward-looking, in the best sense of the word progressive. The direction of this forward movement was towards the child, towards a closer intimacy with his personal, individual purposes and interests.

The whole development of the conception of group work in the English primary school, in spite of the confusions, the delays, the misunderstandings and misinterpretations, the ephemeral fashions, the jargon, the disagreements and generation gaps in staff rooms, has been in one direction and with one purpose: to reduce the distance between teacher and child, to come closer to the learner, and with a greater understanding of the peculiar circumstances, past history, background, difficulties, strengths, weaknesses, motivations and interests of individuals, to be able to minister more appropriately to their social, emotional and intellectual development.

Such an experiment involved a greater number of staff meetings, usually on a weekly basis, to evaluate progress, take stock and plan the next phase of work for groups and individuals. The particular cases of individual children were a prominent feature in these staff discussions and invariably led to modifications of the programme. It is significant that it was this very concern for the educational welfare of individual children that facilitated a further liberation in the use of time and space.

Stage 6   The ultimate in flexibility

The latest stage in this process envisages a maximum of flexibility in the use of time and space. Timetables have tended to disappear, except for adjustments related to the use of the hall. Many new buildings are open-plan with split-level classrooms adapted to the interests and intellectual requirements of groups and individuals. There is no formal arrangement of groups or of furniture.

Another key word, along with flexibility, is availability: availability of resources, books and tools; and availability of the teacher who spends much time in moving about the class from one group to another. Children start work on an interest or subject and work at it until they are ready for a change of activity. A space may not be available in the reading corner, but there is always a wealth of work to be completed, so the child moves to that until he is able to settle into the appropriate work space. This seems to suggest the final abdication and redundancy of the teacher, but nothing could be further from the truth. There is still the perennial problem of organization with children's work now to be mapped at an individual level, occasional group work and classwork to be planned, an environment for learning to be created, resources to be provided, encouragement, praise, guidance and correction to be given to all the children, backward readers to be heard and taught, using a repertoire of made-to-measure apparatus, for, contrary to current rumour, teachers still teach. The initial impact of a story whether from literature or history or the present day, told to the whole class, comes from the teacher, and this too, as well as the occasional school visit, can become a springboard for a multitude of varied group and individual activities. With so much to do and such stimulus for doing it there should be no aimless wandering children.

A suggested recipe for success offered to a nervous beginner in teaching would be to make sure that the climate of the school is favourable and positively committed to flexibility of approach, individualized teaching, integrated learning and mixed-ability grouping, then to work gradually, with three or four groups, with only limited choices to begin with in a carefully prepared environment, and no unnecessary walking about. Where skills are concerned children need concentration on the task in hand with a minimum of distractions, and it is the duty of the teacher to isolate the difficulties in order to eliminate them one by one. Certain times of day are more tranquil than others and the mastery of the various basic skills is more easily achieved at these times. For example, in my experience I found that

.centration on academic subjects was more easily achieved after rather ⨿han before such activities as physical education, games and swimming, but experience differs from one kind of organization to another. Teachers and children have their own personal rhythms of working, and it may take time and a little experimenting to discover the most suitable timing and location for the different kinds of learning. However cautious, tentative and groping these beginnings, the provision of materials and books must be generous, challenges bold and adventurous and encouragement never-ceasing. 'Child-centredness' and 'subject-centredness' are two absurdly unrealistic polarities and the values which they represent are not mutually exclusive, but a teacher who is aware of the prominence of the learner has, in addition to being a reliable authority on subject matter, the sensitive and delicate task of accommodating his academic knowledge and practical skills to his psychological understanding of his pupils. Insight into the nature of children and their behaviour in groups is essential for a teacher, but even a rudimentary knowledge of psychology can confirm that learning is not automatic. Most experienced teachers are aware that every conceivable positive condition for learning and working has to be created. Among such considerations are a child's basic desire to be accepted, his wish to feel secure, his curiosity and craving for adventure and novelty yet within a safe and orderly setting, his longing to be accepted by his peer group and by his teacher, his urge to contribute and to be useful, but above all to achieve and through achievement to win a sense of his own worthwhile identity and to gain acceptance of himself. The teacher's nearness rather than remoteness will be a support in this arduous, upward struggle.

As relationships grow within these more flexible groupings and an atmosphere of security and stability is built up, the range of choices can be extended. Thereafter children will extend them themselves.

It cannot be too strongly emphasized that without the particular, personal gifts and character of the teacher, no mere organization, grouping or methodology can improve the quality of education. The teacher is the kingpin. Where the personal quality of the teacher is good and attitudes to children are positive, sympathetic and attentive, innovations and experiments in class organization and management would be of secondary importance, but might be necessary to enable the good to be better, to help the teacher to improve upon his assets by bringing these good qualities into closer contact with individual children. Of what use is compassion or zeal in the cause of learning if inhibited by an inflexible arrangement of desks, or blocked by a guillotining timetable?

It needs to be said also that, given freedom to manoeuvre, the good teacher will strain every nerve to create, within his sphere of influence, those conditions, environmental, physical, social and emotional, which he believes to be in the best interests of his pupils. This could mean moving the desks, keeping them where they are or abolishing them altogether! The teacher's own personal and professional freedom is therefore of the utmost importance. In many subtle ways, therefore, a teacher's classroom, or work space, will reflect his own educational philosophy and teaching style.

Other groupings of children
There is an endless range of patterns of grouping provided by children at play. No adult has been consulted in this case either to approve or disapprove. Children in such circumstances provide a unique training situation for teachers. Here a young teacher can study at first hand the spontaneous groupings of children that follow upon friendships, interests, skills and individual idiosyncrasies. Left to themselves, children will weave interesting social patterns of their own. For psychological and linguistic as well as social reasons, it is important that children have time to play with their peers. In a multicultural classroom, for example, it is essential that children should have sufficient time in which to practise the arts of communicating with each other. With increased understanding of the learning process it has become glaringly obvious that teaching does not inevitably imply class teaching or even classrooms and schools. In fact, old-fashioned though it seems, class teaching is the latest arrival on the educational scene. It came into its own when church, then state, assumed responsibility for educating the people. Individual tutorials and group discussions go back at least as far as ancient Greece, and there is evidence that they existed in Old Testament times. Now we are trying hard to shake off some of the chains forged more recently in the nineteenth century when the demands of mass teaching made the most truly educative situation of all – the face-to-face meeting of teacher and pupil – look like an impossible dream. Methods and techniques which are adjusted to the flow of sympathy and discovery between teacher and pupil must then be seen to be, not gimmicks or extravagant inventions for sugaring a pill, but natural outcomes of an observed desire to learn. This is where a teacher's creativity comes in, where the science and art of education unite to create conditions which will arouse this desire. Where life itself is generous enough in supplying food for learning there is no need

to whip up temporary enthusiasms by elaborate stunts and changes of fashion. People and places, words and music, numbers and patterns, symbols and shapes, colours and textures, past and present, there is enough material for learning and doing without trying to compete with the world of entertainment.

The above-mentioned stages did not exist in such an oversimplified, separate form, nor in such strict chronological sequence (as some classrooms still perpetuate the formal practices of stage 1), but allowing for many overlaps and the simultaneity of both old and new practices, the idea of stages is used merely as a simple device to describe the general historical trend away from didactic class teaching towards group and individual-orientated teaching.

At the present time patterns of grouping in primary schools have an eclectic quality, ranging from one extreme of almost complete freedom based upon children's interests and choices, to the other extreme of a return to formal arrangements of desks, reflecting both parental pressures and those of the government for a return to standards. This latter picture is not true of all schools, and indicates not an advance but rather a retreat following the much publicized call 'back to the basics', as though basic skills had never been a major concern of teachers in the twentieth century. In fact diversity continues to be the characteristic not only of the schools, but often of methods and class organization within the same school. Given this lack of uniformity, group work, largely determined by the guiding purposes of the teacher, is still the dominant practice in many primary schools where the achievements of former practitioners have been too firmly rooted to be ousted by politicians or the media. Although the present educational climate does not appear to some teachers to be the most favourable one for the adoption of a radically individualized way of working, many, even in their group and class work, are sensitive to the peculiar needs of individual children, and cater for them in different ways. One great advance in the early 1970s and 1980s, in spite of the adverse financial situation, has been the extended use of the environment, the exploration of different neighbourhoods, the number of out-of-school excursions and the greater use of museums and other local and national resources. Another significant feature of the last decade has been the involvement of parents and the community in the work of the school, and the opportunities which all the above developments offer for individual activity and expression (Taylor Report 1977).

Another recent development has been the combining of specialisms in co-operative teaching. Children can still have a home base and a teacher who knows them as individuals, but he may possess talents which children in other classes are allowed to share. Likewise teachers with different gifts can come together and jointly work with other classes as well as their own. The key word is flexibility, particularly in schools which combine co-operative teaching with family grouping. Obviously such a system depends for its success upon the quality of relationships within the school as a whole. The teachers are obliged by the nature of their work to co-operate with each other and to share not only each other's pupils but their resources, their work space and their expertise. Children reap the advantages of being able to get help from more than one teacher, to gain access to more books and material and, in a varied group of mixed ages, to find their own level among a greater variety of children, some of whom are more able and others less able than themselves. The most important gain for the teachers is a greater knowledge of each others' pupils and the consequent ability to share each others' problems concerning the difficulties of individual children.

Some patterns of organization in the teaching of reading and mathematics
Teacher control of group work was at its most precise in the early days of experiment with the teaching of reading and mathematics. The following are two typical schemes of that period, roughly during the 1940s and early 1950s.

Learning to read
Class teaching and 'reading round the class', with the necessity of inflicting the same book on all children simultaneously, was felt by many teachers to be the least productive method of catering for the diversities of ability, interest and speed of performance so that alternative ways had to be found. Apart from valuable discussions of new words encountered in the general area of language, as a result of communal experiences such as excursions, visits, school journeys, environmental studies and stories read aloud or told by the teacher, the attempt to teach reading to a whole class as a learning unit came to be abandoned. It must not be assumed, however, that the study of etymology and word-derivation is beyond the intellectual grasp of juniors or outside the range of their interests. Many children today are fascinated by the ancient world, and are attracted by the surviving traces of

a bygone age. Many of their homes contain relics once in daily use by their grandparents: an old teapot, a curiously shaped jug, an oil lamp or a wheel-backed chair. With such objects, left behind by a previous generation, in mind, children have had their imaginations stirred by the idea of other relics having been left behind by former dwellers in these islands, in the form of words now in everyday use, words of ancient British, Roman, Saxon, Viking and Norman origin. If a child's vocabulary is to be extended, discussion of words with others in a communal setting, and with shared experience as the cue, is as much a justification for drawing all the class together as for the enjoyment of music or poetry. Other more functional, but to some children not necessarily uninteresting aspects of language, such as grammar and spelling, do not have to be banished from the warm climate of 'communal' discussions into the bleak regions of formal exercises. They would benefit from inclusion in the wider area opened up by the growing junior's increasing curiosity about words. Most teachers in primary schools are aware of the younger children's love of rhymes, jingles and chorus work, and the older child's experimenting with tongue-twisters and difficult erudite circumlocutions (I. and P. Opie 1962). Language in all its aspects can be a magic territory for children to explore and no part of it need be dull. In our enthusiasm for creative writing we may have forgotten that some structures and skills involved in human expression and communication have creative and imaginative origins and can be taught creatively. It is mistaken and certainly misleading for children to think that the mother tongue is divisible into two parts, one exciting and one dull, or translated into curriculum phraseology as creative writing on the one hand and comprehension or grammar or spelling on the other. They are all indispensable parts of a mind-expanding whole. Observation of children, the nature of their experience and the topicalities of their everyday lives will prompt the vigilant teacher in choosing the appropriate moment for teaching a relevant aspect of language, sometimes to an individual, sometimes to a small group of individuals and sometimes to the whole class.

Reading for fluency
Class teaching is dead for those kinds of learning which depend upon the individual learner's peculiar way and speed of grasping concepts and mastering skills, but certain kinds of learning can achieve significance and permanence by being enjoyed and shared in common. The emphasis should be on enjoyment. Because the ability to read is a privately won skill, ways of

teaching have had to be explored which were more attuned to the particular nature and circumstances of the learner. The class was therefore broken up into groups according to different levels of attainment. This had the desirable effect of necessitating as many different sets of reading books as possible. These were graded to suit the abilities of the children. It was the custom to have one good reader attached to each group to help the others whenever necessary. The selection of good leaders was essential for success as one of the duties of the group leader was to keep a record of the books read by the group. This method had advantages and disadvantages. It was superior to reading round the class in that it did ensure maximum reading practice for all the children in the class. Some children might read aloud as many as five times during a lesson. The reading material was appropriate to the needs of individuals, and slow readers gained confidence in reading to others whose ability was similar to their own. The teacher was free, not only to supervise the whole class, but also to give attention to backward readers. These children could be helped by being asked to read to the teacher and by being given encouragement to make progress at their own rate. Variety could be introduced into this kind of lesson by the exchange of books with other classes similarly organized. Disadvantages were social and, in the case of the group leaders, intellectual and educational. The individual child's rate of progress and status in the class became common knowledge and might, in the case of struggling readers or sensitive newcomers (especially those of different ethnic origins), lead to discouragement. It could also perpetuate the erroneous idea that reading aloud to an audience was the only possible reading experience, obscuring altogether the main aim of showing reading to be something to be enjoyed silently in private. Another possible disadvantage was the unexplored effect upon the more advanced child, in particular the group leader, who had little opportunity to forge ahead, make progress at his own fast rate, and apart from his social usefulness and sense of fulfilment in helping others, was denied the lonely pleasure of enjoying books for themselves. This was to be compensated for in the silent reading or library periods.

Reading for comprehension
Another kind of group organization associated with the teaching of reading and aimed at helping teachers to evaluate children's understanding of what they read focused attention on comprehension. Children were given questions on cards about selected passages of reading material. It was important

that answers be assessed not as evidence of a retentive memory so much as of the ability to grasp the meaning of the printed word. Questions were being aimed at giving a purpose and a direction to the reading, so both questions and text were exposed together. No attempt was made to conceal the reading matter while the questions were being answered, otherwise the exercise became a memory test. Words may mean different things to different children, so in order that a teacher might diagnose any difficulty a child might have in understanding either meaning or symbol, and ascertain what meaning or lack of meaning the appearance of a word might have to individuals, no clues to pronunciation or meaning were to be given by having the passage read aloud. One child, for example, might read 'mizzled' for misled, so in order to detect individual misinterpretations the reading must be silent and the questions answered in writing.

Reading for pleasure
With this isolation of the various objectives and aspects of reading for the purpose of mastering the skill there was a tendency to think of reading for pleasure as only one other kind of reading lesson with different aims from those of other reading experiences. In more formal schools the enjoyment of books was not so much an aim as a reward for achievement in the formal reading lesson, and a holiday for the teacher who was thereby released from teaching. It was therefore banished to a separate period on the timetable, known as a library period, often to a different room proudly referred to as the library, and at its worst to be the privilege enjoyed only by the best readers or as a special concession.

It was, however, during this artificially segregated period of reading for pleasure that many teachers gained their best insights into the teaching of reading and, indeed, into the nature of education itself. They became skilful in selecting books for the library along the lines of children's interests, and in this they were helped by the steadily increasing volume of reviews of books for children appearing in the daily press and in teachers' journals throughout the 1950s and 1960s, and by the growing number of writers of quality in this market of children's literature. In this same enterprise of catering for the growing curiosity of young minds teachers endeavoured to make available and easily accessible all the necessary resources in the form of attractive and widely ranging book corners in their own classrooms. With such plentiful provision readily to hand, the choice belongs to the individual child and books themselves become agents in the loosening and breaking-up of rigid classroom structures. There is no need now to sit in groups or, in fact, in any particular pattern of seating. Comfort should be the best condition in which to derive most pleasure and profit from reading. Any technique which will lead to the enjoyment of books and enhance interest in reading is earnestly sought after. Any device which dulls interest is avoided. So teachers did not test children in this lesson and did not set exercises, neither did they discourage discussion or questions which arose out of their pleasure reading. These gave rise to an enjoyable social get-together at the end of the period. Some exercises, however, children did enjoy in connection with their own chosen reading. These included giving reviews of books which they had particularly enjoyed or reading exciting extracts aloud to the class or dramatizing suitable episodes. Every child was encouraged to keep a personal diary of books read.

Grouping according to mixed aims within the reading period
Another kind of organization evolved from these experiments with the different aims of the reading lesson: reading for fluency, comprehension (as if one should ever read without comprehension) and pleasure, until now (the late 1940s and early 1950s) all treated separately. This was to allow for all three kinds of lesson to proceed simultaneously, with one or two groups having practice sessions for fluency, another group answering questions in writing from cards and another group reading for their own private pleasure. One advantage of this was again on the side of the teacher who was thus free to give help to individuals where it was most needed. Rotation of groups in succeeding sessions was to ensure a fair distribution of the different reading activities and experiences.

In this brief look at the development of group methods in the teaching of reading we have arrived at the stage in the history of group work where children are engaged in a variety of activities, but all of these are still related to one subject. This slow evolution applies to the curriculum of the junior school, for in the infant school upon which the observation and research of the early pioneers had been mainly focused, liberalization of the young child's learning programme and working day had been proceeding at a faster rate.

As we have seen, the next stage in the development of junior education was marked by a kind of organization, sometimes found in rural schools where numbers were small and material and books were scarce, which experimented with the idea of different groups engaged in different subjects at the same time. Teachers were learning that children could be trusted when interested and responsible, and that teachers with such a way of working were freer to give individual attention. At this point it is appropriate to look at a parallel process occurring in the teaching of mathematics (formerly limited to arithmetic) in the junior school.

Learning mathematics

The break-up of the class lesson in mathematics occurred in a small way at first to give children a chance to see the relevance of arithmetic to everyday life, and to engage in some practical activity. This was invariably the shop where only small groups of children, four in the group at most, took it in turns to be shopkeepers and customers when money was the topic of the lesson. The rest of the class remained at their desks doing formal sums. But the practical work was not restricted to shopping. Weighing, measuring and estimating all involved, for one small group at a time at least, moving out of their seats and doing practical work. More enterprising teachers took their children outside to measure the playground, but then this was a class activity, carefully controlled by the use of detailed assignments.

More adventurously still, teachers in the mathematics lesson reached the same stage in group work which they were reaching in reading and had already reached in art and physical education: groups doing different things at the same time but all activities still closely related to the subject designated on the timetable. The number of groups increased with the diversity of work in mathematics, as knowledge of the range and compass of mathematical thinking itself grew and captured the imagination of teachers: one group of children might be practising the skills of basic number as this foundation work must still go on. Revision of previously learned processes was essentially *re*-vision, looking again at a familiar scene from a different angle, subtraction in the light of addition, division undivorced from multiplication and mathematics seen as another kind of language, having obvious links with history, geography, science and the symbol-using arts of calligraphy and music.

Another group of children might be engaged in problems, puzzles and mathematical games where the relation to language was clear, as many of the answers might be in the form of words rather than figures. Problems would relate to the experiences and trials of every day. Travelling at a given speed in a car which breaks down, followed by an enforced walk to the station, interrupted by the kind offer of a lift from a friendly neighbour, travelling at a different and necessarily faster speed; did Mr. Jones catch his train after all? The answer would be Yes or No. Though the mental operations were mathematical, the answer came as part of a conversation between child and teacher.

Then another group would be involved in such practical activities as drawing, measuring, weighing, counting, estimating heights or doing experiments with dice on chance and probability or classifying and sorting objects into sets.

A fourth group could be engrossed in constructive work involving estimation and calculation: making a bird table, a cage for a hamster or gerbil, designing a geometrical model as a lampshade or building a weather station.

A fifth group might be studying the history of mathematics, with mental excursions into ancient Egypt, Babylon, Greece or Rome. Out of this would come other activities besides specifically mathematical ones: making travel books to go along with models of the Pyramids, making a sundial and various kinds of ancient time-pieces, including candle and water clocks, experiments with a home-made pendulum, taking a clock to pieces, tracing the history of speed through the compared performances of children in the classroom, adult pedestrians, athletes, horses, bicycles, cars, ships, balloons, aeroplanes and rockets, followed by the making of charts and the dismantling of a speedometer.

Such a variety of possible activities within the field of mathematics invariably led to a more flexible treatment of the subject, growing out of children's interests and conversation, their comments and questions, from the varied collections of objects and from local and topical investigations. This was the period when the variety of activities was still contained within the area considered proper to that particular subject. Flexibility of groupings, embracing individual work as well, had arrived but it was not yet total. Changing attitudes to mathematics as being, like language, an inescapable fact of life have led to classrooms where diverse activities are seen to exist side by side, and the extension of the age range from junior to middle school has enlarged the area of difficulty and achievement in children's mathematical development.

Choice of learning material

With so much public interest focused upon what is actually learned in school, and the call, on the part of some authorities, for a common core curriculum, it is timely to look at the progress of the curriculum in the primary school during the twentieth century and to try to understand the reasons for the direction which it has taken in the last five decades. With the advantage of hindsight it is now clear that choice of learning material followed the same direction of reducing the distance between teacher and child as can be noticed in the evolution of classroom groupings and organization, from the one extreme of instruction given arbitrarily on the basis of what the teacher considered to be the next step on the ladder of learning, a linear approach dictated by a school or examination syllabus, to the other extreme of learning attendant upon the observed interests of children.

If formal education is to be considered worthwhile only if it can serve the vocational ambitions of individuals or the economic, industrial or militaristic aims of the state, then it loses its own essential character – that of being worthwhile for its own sake. It should perhaps best be called schooling rather than education. Teachers need to be convinced of the intrinsic value of education apart from any advantage which this might have in the furthering of other aims, vocational, social or national. A teacher who has this degree of confidence in education itself is an enthusiastic teacher and a true professional. Such professional excitement is a quality which children should expect to find in those responsible for their education. The worth of education is essentially in what it does for people as individuals (because its effects can only be induced and experienced at a personal, individual level, given the diversity of human beings) and consequently for the community which such educated individuals create. The forward march of primary education in the twentieth century has been due, neither to a submission to the pressures of the state, nor to the neglect of the legitimate claims of society, but to an increasingly closer attention to the educational potential of individual children (including the handicapped). Society cannot but be a beneficiary when its individual members are achieving their maximum growth.

Where the immediate task of choosing not only suitable but necessary learning material is concerned, as always in education an oversimplified and exclusive adherence to any one approach is rarely found, and there have been the inevitable intermediate stages where teachers were at pains to discover themes which they thought to be both interesting to children and in the educational interests of children. Without going as far back as the late nineteenth century when the emphasis in elementary education was upon basic reading, writing and arithmetic, and assuming the fundamental requirements, both for individual fulfilment and for social competence, of literacy (including confident, expressive speech) and numeracy, and accepting the welcome additions of music and the expansion of pencil-drawing sessions into the wider opportunities of art, and drill metamorphosed into physical education, there remained a vast area of knowledge and skill unexplored except by reference to children's own experience, curiosity and interests. This is the area so often referred to in autobiographies as having been completely ignored and neglected in the writers' schooldays, the world of wonder, exploration and excitement entered only privately or with a chosen friend during long summer holidays: rambles in the country, exploring the life of woodland and stream and seashore, excursions into the past in museums or city streets, experiments with a magnifying glass or microscope, a solitary raid on a library and the lonely discovery of the world of books.

The intermediate stage, before teachers in any large numbers felt it possible, profitable or safe to leave the choice of subject matter to children themselves, dates, for the majority of primary schools, from the years immediately following the Second World War and continues up to the present day with odd excursions into the realm of free choice and an occasional harking back to more authoritarian times. During this time topics for study have been pursued according to any one or combinations of the following reasons which could be identified as logical or psychological, and further subdivided the reasons might fit into categories which, without being too rigid and exclusive, could be called sequential, topical, environmental, seasonal, personal or accidental. None of these categories excludes the others but each word merely designates the main source of inspiration for each area of study. It is worth noting that, at least as far as primary education was concerned, there was a departure from the traditional subject labels and consequently an opening for a more integrated approach to knowledge based upon the learner's own experiences and interests.

Can any particular learning matter be described as necessary, either for the educational health of the individual or the proper functioning of the society to which the individual belongs? Must all school learning be based on interests? The answer to this question demands an appeal to philosophy and requires a whole book to itself (which in fact has already been written: P. S. Wilson 1971). A short answer to the question might be that schools in various ways have attempted to base their programmes on children's interests and at the same time upon learning material which has been considered to be in the interests of children. Both kinds of work involve the concept of discipline.

Work that is sequential usually includes those studies that are considered necessary since by definition they involve those skills and abilities the achievement of which depends upon the mastery of graded processes in a certain order. There are certain aspects of mathematics, language and music, for example, which cannot be grasped without a previous understanding of earlier steps. One immediately thinks of an attempt to add tens before being able to add units, but, more mistakenly it was thought impossible for children to be able to read without first knowing the letters of the alphabet. This was sequential thinking at its most blind, and the alphabetic method of teaching reading was one of the earliest and the most illogical. Now it is commonplace for some children, even skipping the whole word approach, to come to reading through the medium of simple sentences aided by a meaningful context and pictures. What the right sequence is is not always possible to determine in the absence of the child who is to be taught. In fact research has shown that children grasp concepts of space before those of number (Piaget and Inhelder 1956), which would seem to suggest that simple geometrical ideas, together with some practical and constructional work, might well be introduced before the study of arithmetic, as it used to be called. Musicians might argue that, for example, it is impossible to play the piano without practising scales or that it is out of order to play the third position of fingering on the violin before mastering the first. These arguments sound reasonable but there are equally sound arguments for letting children experiment with the different resonances of strings and keys and wooden blocks in the same way that they are allowed to splash about in water before learning to swim. This raises the whole question of the most profitable use of a child's time in school, the function of the curriculum and the status of sequential learning within it. For a child who comes from a noisy, distracting environment, a whole hour spent in quietly painting a picture (e.g., Peter's fish) might be his very first experience of willing, concentrated attention, and his first awareness that such voluntary attention to a single, purposeful activity can be enjoyable and fulfilling – an experience which could have value for the rigours of other academic areas of the curriculum. To learn to give attention at all is the first and most essential requirement of a student, however young he might be.

The idea of a proper sequence in learning sounds sensible but it can be overdone. Observation of children learning leads one to sense that there is a natural rhythm of learning peculiar to the individual. Traditionally the very notion of history has presupposed that teaching must begin with the remote past and work towards the present day. From the point of view of the young child who has been in the world for only seven or eight years, it would seem not only psychologically but logically defensible to begin the study of history from the present and proceed backwards into the past, from the familiar to the unfamiliar. Indeed the idea of presenting historical material chronologically to children with an undeveloped sense of time could be quite mistaken. A more fruitful approach might be through the association of ideas linked to experiences, such as a visit to a church or castle, or a collection of stones or old clothes. This is another application of the finding that new learning must make a link with previous experience.

Topical events have been a stand-by for many a school or class project, from Halloween, Guy Fawkes' Night or Christmas, to the Olympic Games, the World Cup, the Queen's Jubilee or the local Library Week. It would be interesting to take a census of the number of witches adorning the walls of junior school classrooms during the last week of October. Still bearing in mind the direction of primary school organization and work choices towards a closer proximity to the learning child, one is bound to say that many themes chosen from topical events are heavily teacher-inspired and teacher-directed. Admittedly the quality and variety of work and the enthusiasm generated offer much to be admired, in drawing on a wealth of carefully guided and related activities including drama, movement, music, art, writing and what used to be called social studies, which embraced history and geography.

If immediacy is one advantage of a topical approach, it is conceivable that learning based upon the local environment of school and home neighbourhood, as well as environmental studies proper, could move nearer to the everyday experiences of children than either work based upon a more distant social, national or international happening, or work dictated by an adult concept of what comes next in logical sequence. When compared with adult logic children's associations of ideas, limited as they are by the experiences of a short life-span, appear illogical and at times irrational. A child's account of a visit to a museum may completely ignore the essential points of the excursion, as conceived by the teacher, in strictly educational or archaeological terms, and highlight instead the joys of the bus ride or the unfamiliar thrills of the escalator. The teacher who feels disappointed by this has forgotten that in a hundred years' time both bus and escalator will have become part of archaeology (not to mention the school itself!). Associations of ideas are so personal that any attempt to develop topic work as a class enterprise must inevitably call upon the different experiences and interests of individuals. This does not mean that thirty children will necessarily be doing thirty irreconcilably different things, but that thirty children (preferably twenty or fifteen in an ideal world), some of whose interests and experiences coincide, can contribute, either as individuals or in small groups of like-minded workers, to a large group experience, such as a school or class outing or a story. In topic work of this kind, involving individual choices, with children exploring approved interests of their own, it is good to remember that they are still members of a group. It is therefore important both for the group and the individual that opportunity is given for the experiences of each child to be shared by all, with the teacher in control drawing maximum substance and sustenance from each interest as it develops. There is a rhythm of going out and coming in, but it may not necessarily be contained within the confines of one lesson. The younger the children the more frequent will be the return to the centre, to the teacher, for reassurance, encouragement, guidance and further teaching. As pupils grow older the ebb and flow of the tide will be over an ever-widening area, and over longer periods of time, like the investigations of research workers gathering facts for a government report, collecting evidence, interviewing witnesses. In such a situation it is vital for the advancement of knowledge that the findings are brought back to the centre for further examination and discussion. Then the learners go out again and explore further and deeper. It is the teacher who usually (but not always) initiates the step further, helps in the shedding of new light, gives more encouragement and supplies fresh material. The going out on a solitary quest may simply be reading a book in the quiet of a library or the silent operation of original thinking, or it may be literally climbing a mountain. The coming back to the centre is talking about one's experiences and reporting discoveries which may be physical or intellectual or emotional ones, or mixtures of all three. Such a rhythm of venturing out, coming back, of scattering and converging is valid for education at any level. It takes account of individual abilities, personal tastes and the inspiration derived from group membership.

Some orderly minded teachers, upset by the apparent lack of congruent thinking in children, attempt to impose their own mental structures upon the child's work plan, so we have this kind of development of a topic starting in approved style from the child's own environment, the subject being a domestic pet: our cat. The scrupulous teacher suggests the following radiating pattern:

Cat

1 What is cat a part of? The cat family. What does this include? The lion, tiger, leopard, cheetah, puma. A visit to the zoo is indicated.

2 What are the parts of a cat? Claws, whiskers, fur . . . To take only claws as an example. These are defences. Develop this idea. Other defences. How other animals defend themselves: fangs, poison, horns, camouflage. How man defends himself: fists and feet (Kung-fu!), innumerable weapons (this will please the boys, thinks the teacher), and protection through the ages, fortresses, castles, gunpowder (topical for 5th November), battleships, submarines, tanks, bombers. It becomes obvious that if you start anywhere in the universe you can get anywhere, because the resourceful teacher knows that all things are related. With some ingenuity it is even possible with the aid of a 'Project' to get back to the old familiar formal lesson. 'Progressive' educators have therefore tended to become increasingly suspicious of the too tidy project however embellished with impressive model-making.

3 What are the qualities of a cat? Adjectives galore, smooth, silky, sleek, relaxed, comfort-loving, wily, artful, clever, independent, mysterious, inscrutable, nocturnal, bewitching . . . leading on to the reading of poems and the writing of verse and prose.

4 Associations of ideas. What does cat remind you of? There is obviously a greater freedom here to dilate the area of personal experience and reminiscence: our dog, the fishmonger and the milkman, Dick Whittington, mice, rats, the Pied Piper . . .

5 Doing things with the topic under discussion: how to look after a cat.

Is there anything wrong with this carefully planned approach? The teacher has started from a topic based firmly within a child's own environment, experience and interest, and a careful plan covering the ground is surely better than no plan at all. It is also true that excellent results in terms of finished products have been achieved in this way to the delight of parents on open days. It is also true that some children appear to require more direction than others. Nevertheless it is true, too, if one must mention public or semi-public displays of children's work, that the too-visible hand of the teacher, who, as has already been emphasized, must always be the creator and sustainer, in the background, can have a deadening effect both on a child's initial excitement and curiosity and, in an unmistakably identifiable way, on the final product. There is a moment in the life of an enthusiastic teacher when the plan takes over. It must drag through to its logical conclusion, cover every step, unaware that the child is not going along with it, having stopped on the way to stare at some other irrelevant enchantment. This raises the whole question of direction. The term 'teacher-directed' is sometimes used in a derogatory way to denote an approach which stifles the natural spontaneity of children. But there are various kinds of direction. To have a sense of direction facilitated by a few clear and beguiling signposts is a desirable condition for learners as well as for travellers, and is very different from having all the wonder and romance of the journey killed by being instructed in every step of the way. It is a mistaken notion that it is the duty of a teacher to give the world to the child with the supposition that the child is in one place and the world is in another. In one sense the child is in the world. In another sense the world is within the child. Research, both sociological and psychological, has demonstrated how intimately a child is linked to his own immediate world and to the whole universe of space, shape, colour, sound, time and movement (Piaget 1929, 1950, 1952, 1956). There is no right order for the presentation of these experiences, for by the time a child has reached school age they are parts of his own being. The ordering and analysing of experience, important as these are, must wait upon experience itself. How joyous this can be when, with an observant teacher as the provider, one is free to choose! So the teacher has not been banished from the scene. Through knowledge of his pupils he strives to ensure their active mental involvement which is a necessary condition for learning. The teacher as provider is a key concept. Provision of material resources, tools and equipment, the very colour and warmth of the environment itself, together with provision of guidance and opportunity for activity and discovery come from the teacher. The perceptive teacher starts observantly and attentively (as a good observer and a good listener) from the child's world (wider now than it used to be if one thinks of television and modern travel) and extends it. One obvious extension is towards others in the community of which the school is a thoughtful part, and children should be given early experience of caring relationships with vulnerable human beings, the very young, the old and the handicapped. Religious education could find a meaningful beginning here. Within the Christian tradition harvest festivals and Christmas provide for some schools opportunities for regular links with the local hospital or old people's home. In general, identification with a school usually means identification with moral and social values (Shipman 1975, Pluckrose 1979).

Work with a seasonal inspiration can embrace both topical and environmental themes though the emphasis is on the rhythm of life itself and on the natural world. How empty the modern primary school classroom would look without its usual collections of spring and summer flowers and autumn leaves! A visit to a farm can combine environmental interests and seasonal activities. Sequence comes into its own here, and it is especially important for innercity children, considering how short their primary school life is, not only to learn about, but in various ways, through excursions into all conceivable open spaces, parks, canal banks and legally approved visits to railway sidings, even churchyards, to experience the inevitable procession of the seasons and come back to school with a collection of treasures to arrange and mount and talk about. How else can a child in a concrete environment be aware of the subtle changes that take place in nature with the passing of a school year? How can he make sense of books which talk about soil or of poems about squirrels? One nine-year-old boy who lived in Deptford had never seen the river, or indeed any river. The very word Deptford implies river.

Every season has its own particular enchantment for children, and winter has its special joys. The arrival of snow offers a creative opportunity not to be missed, whether in the town, as in an example from Adrian, in London, or in the country with Christopher, Colin, Christine and Carolyn.

A Snowy Day in London

Now the snow is falling in small flakes, gradually increasing. Now the people at the bus stop are stamping their shoes to get the cold out. Now the bus slowly crawls up the slushy grey roads, with the ice and slush caked to it, half an hour late. Now as it gets dark, there is only a boy running home, with his cold blue hands and a scarf round his neck. Now as the last bus comes crawling round, everything is quiet. Silent, only the slush pushed to one side dripping into the drains.

Adrian (aged 11)

November Snow

Giants had drawn white blankets over the countryside.
At dawn things had changed.
It was different, it had snowed.
Tidal wave after tidal wave the snow fell
Cascading down in a million little diamonds.
It was snow in November.
Everything in its path it smothered
The rooftops white.
There was snow on cars windscreens
And the windows are frosted.
It was snow in November.

Christopher (aged 10)

Winter at Coxley

A wintery summer day we went down Coxley today.
We noticed that the grass and fields were bitter and bleached with the cold frosty days.
The hedgese had withered away.
A stream ran down the path then went down a slope.
The hedgese of the field were swampy indeed.
The stream at Coxley came down a small waterfall rushing under the bridge and hurling through like mad.
There was a dead bird on a swampy part of bank.
The wheather was nice but chilly.

Colin (aged 8)

The End of Winter

All the path were gleemy and wet, sludgy and moist and very sloshy.
The weather was cold with the sun out a little.
The bushes were shiny and still bristly with slender branches were rustling away with a sliver of cold. Fields had been bitten from the frost.
The birds twittered and sang after each other.
The silvery bubles began to burst a little from the stream.
There were thousands of stones with grayish colours.

Christine (aged 8)

Snow

The snow fell
In big flakes,
Crisp and white,
Standing still,
Shaking silently
Down, down, down.

Upon the trees,
Upon the grass,
Making everything
Still, smooth, clean,
Like white silk
Of a lady's
Wedding dress.

It shimmers through
Branches of bare trees
And glistens on
The clear ice of ponds.
But still
Silver and soft,
Smooth and silky
Lies snow.

Carolyn (aged 8)

Seasonal activities expressed in writing, art, music and drama also find an appropriate place in learning about religious faiths and festivals, especially in a multicultural classroom, and provide opportunities for the sharing of diverse experiences.

Personally based topics leave the door wide open for individual idiosyncrasy, whether of child or teacher: our holiday by the seaside, my sister's wedding, my baby brother, Spain in the summer, travel by air, my collection of train numbers, my chemistry set, the microscope grandpa gave me, budgerigars; the list is endless. The following are two examples of interests near to home:

My Daddy in the War

You had to be 19 (I think) to be in the Army and at the time of the war, the Army needed all the young men. Daddy was one of them. It was the Second World War – it began in 1939 and it lasted five years, but Daddy was only in it four years because the fifth year, he had a holiday.

Daddy was in the Royal Artillery. Larkhill is the School of Artillery and is open to the public twice every year. Last year, we went when it was open to the public. There was an electronic compass and Daddy tested his prismatic compass (which is an oil compass) and it was right! The men in the Army sent messages by use of walky-talky radio receiving sets. Some use some of the same parts for sending and receiving. On the microphone they have a button, and when you press it there is a loud sound like air passing through the head-phones, very fast, but it really the electricity passing through without any other parts to make the sound vibrations. The gunners used walky-talky to tell them in which direction to shoot.

Each soldier had to obey orders and be truthful and brave. Sometimes they died from cold and discomfort and only a ¼ of them are left and in towns and villages they are in urgent need of people to work in offices and places like that. For all the men (or nearly) are dead. My Daddy survived.

Mark (aged 7)

The following description, by another Mark, shows how fluent an eleven-year-old can be when dealing with something well within his personal experience.

Our Cat

Our cat is very tall and slender. He walks cautiously as if prepared for anything. His green eyes are like emeralds. His nose is always very moist and his fur is black and beautiful and shines like glossy black paint. Usually when we are eating an evening meal our cat jumps up on the window ledge outside. He walks up and down, then eventually he stops and looks at us. Occasionally he opens his little mouth and lets out a penetrating miaow and he looks pitifully at us as we eat. At last Mother lets him in. Then he goes straight to his food, looks at it as if it is not what he wants, then trots away proudly and leaps like a tiger up the stairs where he settles down on someone's bed. Later on in the evening he slowly walks down the stairs and into our back room where the fire is. He moves cautiously towards the fire. When he feels the warmth he collapses in a ball with his little nose under his paw.

Liver is a thing our cat is very fond of. Whenever liver is around he is always hungry. He seems to talk to you by what he looks like. He usually looks very pitiful. When he is outside, he rolls over on the pavement and if he sees me he turns over quickly and looks at me in a funny way, then he arches his back and walks away. . . .

One needs to remember, too, that where the personal interests of juniors are concerned one is not limited to the narrow world of home and hobbies. There are many children whose interests are academic and coincide with those of the teacher. There are possibly more excited mathematicians and scientists of junior school age than colleagues in the secondary school are aware of, and this sometimes regardless of ability, as in the case of a slow-learning girl who made a working model of a mineshaft to help her to understand positive and negative numbers (plus above ground, minus below ground), or the children who in their making of model boats were trying to demonstrate the relationship between speed and the shape of the vessel.

Topics that arise by accident are very often the fruit of alert observation on the part of either teacher or child, as in the case of the book made by children about the thrush with the broken wing which alighted in the playground and was adopted and looked after by the class, or the February floods which inundated part of the school grounds, resulting in the making of an ingenious bridge by the children, or the swarm of bees which visited a school in North Kensington, or the following poem written by David about the trees felled to make room for the building of the new cloakrooms:

> *On Seeing Trees Cut Down*
> Poor trees
> Poor birds
> Poor leaves
> The old trees have been cut down
> The nests are broken
> The leaves are brown and withered.
>
> Poor branch
> Poor trunk
> Poor twigs
> The branches are cracked and broken
> The trunk has lost its sap
> And the twigs are no more.
>
> Trees, branch, trunk, twigs and leaves
> They have gone to earth
> The birds have flown away.
>
> David (aged 8)

Some wayward, gipsy spirits in the teaching profession, sensitive to every atmospheric change, derive great pleasure from extracting the utmost meaning out of the accidental, the chance comment or awkward question of a child, the strange object picked up on the heath or washed up by the river. They delight in seeing what a wealth of learning can be gleaned from ingenious arrangements of fortuitous happenings and otherwise useless waste material. One group of students found an ancient sword behind the fireplace of an empty house which was in the process of being demolished. Another group, investigating the bed of the River Thames at low tide, found, among an assortment of rubbish, such diverse items as old tiles, some long-stemmed clay pipes under Southwark Bridge and, near Queenhithe, part of an Elizabethan glass bottle, checked as such at the London Museum.

There are many educative by-products which come not only to children but to adults in a closer look at the possibilities of discarded objects, not the least of them being a re-entry into the forgotten world of childhood, a world in which a wooden clothes peg is cherished more than an expensive doll and an iron coat hook becomes the handle which drives a train. Re-arrangements of shapes become invitations to experiment. Recognition of the potentialities of an object is transformed into a conscious purpose. Looking at the possibilities together stimulates the imagination of both adult and child, and provokes discussion, culminating in creation.

Aesthetic awareness is sharpened as shapes or colours arise which either please or displease. No oddment escapes the eye or the hand of the budding artist: lengths of string or wool, buttons, nails or tins. Few activities with paints, inks or other coloured liquids are exempt from pictorial use, whether dropping, dripping, splashing, spraying or smearing. Experiments with different textures or crumpled or folded materials, with rolling logs or flattened leaves can produce striking patterns when used for printing. For the teacher who is artistically aware, surfaces exist to be rubbed: floorboards, wooden planks, unplastered walls, tyres, ornamental glass, coarse linen, wire-mesh, grating or rush-matting.

For three-dimensional effects various shapes can be pressed into clay and there are innumerable uses for sand, plaster and water. All our earlier childhood vices with blots and runny paints now become virtues, and the chance which produces the unexpected beauty of merging colours can be explored further and produced intentionally.

Teachers who find a meaningful place for accidental happenings in their work with children seldom overlook the educational possibilities of the chance find or random adventure. Chance unaided does not make teachers creative, but it does at least furnish them with some opportunities to show their creative talent.

The knowledge explosion
Even when the teacher, after many trials, has become a skilful organizer, and is both adept and sensitive in the choice of learning material that is creative and appropriate to the needs of the children, he may still feel inadequate when faced with the comprehensive nature of his task, to take only the cognitive aspect. Many teachers consider that it is their professional duty, not only to stimulate enthusiasm and set the scene for learning, but also to be experts in dispensing knowledge. One of the immediate

problems pressing upon the primary school is that of the explosion of knowledge due to the scale and rapidity of scientific and technological advance in the twentieth century, especially as its teachers are expected to be competent in every school subject and fully familiar with new developments in all of them. The task of specialists has been described as knowing more and more about less and less. In today's world the teacher in a primary school has to know more and more about more and more, not only with regard to the official sources of knowledge but also to be able to compete at least on equal terms with the expanding knowledge and interests of children.

The Hadow Report of 1931 states, 'the curriculum is to be thought of in terms of activity and experience rather than of knowledge to be acquired and facts to be stored'. Most teachers today recognize the importance of first-hand experience. Some teachers are also willing to grant that, in order to explore and discover the knowledge they need to solve their problems, children should be helped to draw upon the store of knowledge that there is. This giving of knowledge is thought of as an appropriate and timely feeding in of nourishment by a teacher who knows his craft and knows the child. These teachers feel that the distinction between freedom and licence operates in the area of knowledge as in the area of behaviour. Not any old knowledge or any old behaviour will do. One kind of teacher maintains that the child should be free to discover, but that the teacher knows the most fruitful avenues of exploration, the right books to read and the most rewarding treasures that are to be found. Science in the primary school requires more than goodwill.

Other teachers would quarrel with this point of view. They would say that children have their own goals and motivations, their own paths to these goals and can spring the most exciting surprises upon their teachers, who in their turn learn more about children and education as a result and raise their sights accordingly. With such expectations of unpredictability the teacher comes to school prepared to be surprised and accepts that he can't enjoy any surprises if he knows all the answers. It must be conceded that the quality of children's contributions to knowledge depends upon the setting, the stimulus, the motivation, the encouragement and the resources available. All these good things are presumably provided by the teacher. In no case is there abdication by the teacher from the role of provider. Extreme positions obscure important parts of the truth, and the art of school teaching resides in the creation of a community in which members, of which the teacher is one, contribute freely of their gifts and abilities. There are many occasions when leadership, however unobtrusive, discretion and constructive criticism, virtues usually associated with adults, are called for. The Plowden Report (1967) supports the call for activity and experience in the primary school made by the Hadow Report (1931), but adds that knowledge 'is an essential of being educated'. It repudiates the fear that the modern primary school approach leads to the neglect of the older virtues associated with knowledge and maintains that it lays a much firmer foundation for their development.

An analysis of the concept of knowledge is beyond the scope of this book and requires separate treatment (Hirst 1965), but at least a hint of the primary school teacher's problem when faced with all the subjects of the curriculum on the one hand and the knowledge explosion on the other can be glimpsed by considering the following few questions: Is knowledge only something that can be expressed in verbal statements? Must these necessarily be factual statements? Can poetry, for example, not give as valuable a statement about reality as scientific prose? Is not the experience called knowing larger than any spoken or written statement?

Some kinds of knowledge can only be communicated by direct experience, and experience is an individual possession. If one can think of knowledge as increased awareness, then the arts, travel and personal relationships have a considerable contribution to make. So, the knowledge explosion comes about not only because of a rapidly changing world with increasingly widening horizons of human achievement, and because of the increase and range of the means of communication through the mass media, paperback books and other printed publications. It is occasioned not only by the spread of education through the welfare state, but also by the broadening of the concept of knowledge itself. It is this larger idea of knowledge that the Plowden Report was championing, to counteract any misunderstanding of Hadow's 'knowledge to be acquired and facts to be stored'.

With so much knowledge to cope with, a primary school teacher has to look at the value of knowledge, for it comes at all levels and with different motivations. There is the everyday knowledge for immediate practical use: knowing what to do when a tyre is punctured or a fuse is blown. There is the instrumental kind of knowledge used in the service of an art or a craft: what kind of paintbrush will produce this kind of texture? (In the first place it wasn't a paintbrush, it was a knife together with a sponge, in the second place it wasn't paint but wax, and in the third place it was put not on canvas or paper but on cork.) What positioning of the fingers will produce this quality of tone?

Another kind of knowledge is for productivity, and this implies an emphasis on quantity, economy and speed, whether one produces motor cars, sports trophies or examination results. There is knowledge as a possession, leading to greater social status either within an occupational or professional group or within a community.

A more disinterested form of knowledge is that which becomes a step towards more knowledge, a self-perpetuating process. Mathematicians learn and master mathematics in order to learn more mathematics. This fact needs to be grasped by those teachers and students who think only in terms of the social uses of mathematics. In this context knowledge can be thought of as a mental game, for delight, for leisure, for personal enrichment, for fun.

Finally, knowledge can be considered as a process, continuous with growth, though not automatic like maturation, but nevertheless an ongoing, never-ending development: knowing, a verb, rather than knowledge, the noun. Bruner (1970) suggests that any school subject or curriculum area can be translated into activity; he talks of *doing* history, mathematics and physics, thus emphasizing the active, dynamic nature of learning. Education itself needs to be thought of, not as a commodity to be bought, a possession to be prized for its bargaining power, a *thing* which one person has and another has not, but an activity of self-propulsion (to be observed in schools for the mentally handicapped as well as in university laboratories).

In the light of this broad and varied picture of knowledge, how does a teacher in a primary school today cope with all that he is expected to know? How does he compete with television? How does he answer the modern child's serious and increasingly complex questions?

The young teacher's first step is to accept the fact that he can't know it all, that we live in a world in which rapid changes inevitably involve new knowledge to deal with them. Space research in the 1950s, heart surgery in the 1960s, silicon chips in the 1970s are only a few areas in which the boundaries of human knowledge have been extended. All such developments affect education either directly or indirectly. It is interesting to think that one immediate result of the Russian invention of the Sputnik was the return to more formal education on the American scene, in the context of knowledge for productivity.

As a teacher one can learn from the individual child what knowledge is meaningful and of interest to him. Is a teacher justified in condemning the vast store of train numbers in the mind of a junior boy as useless lumber, like the miscellaneous collection of objects in his pockets? There is knowledge which clutters and knowledge which connects, in the sense that it makes connections with structures already built in the mind. Whitehead, as long ago as 1932, talked of the undesirability of inert ideas. Piaget (1950) described the stages of growth of mental structures, the consolidation of one being the necessary foundation for the formation of the next. The valuable knowledge is that which connects, that is part of the growth process. Observation of children reveals that, when highly motivated, they make their own connections in thought, in word and in action. This was exemplified by the group of boys at the play centre who built their own 'shanty town' out of odd pieces of wood, glass and empty petrol cans, borrowed their fathers' tools, even carpenters' aprons, to do the job properly, talked endlessly and obsessively about their task, read magazines about building sheds and ended up cooking sausage suppers enjoyed in their own home-made dens. Teachers can observe the same motivating process at work in children engaged in individual projects, environmental studies and school journeys, or simply at play.

When a teacher discovers the kind of knowledge which does connect, the main problem is to teach children to learn how to learn. This involves a number of conditions, the first of which is that children have sufficient ability to learn. It is remarkable what can be achieved by teachers in special schools for handicapped children, given the encouragement, the materials and the social climate for learning. It is important that children have a variety of experiences to draw from in order to exercise choice, and that resources for learning (books, material, tools and equipment) are available. It is advisable too that children have freedom to learn within an ordered framework, that they have time to think, time to plan and find out for themselves and time to come to their own conclusions without the interruptions of a bell, a clock, a timetable or an examination.

This presupposes individualized methods with a teacher who has a clear vision of education and has established a purposeful and happy climate of learning in the classroom. Personal relationships are fundamental. Social climate involves freedom of access to the teacher, freedom of discussion, natural ways of talking to each other and sharing of ideas and materials with other children of different ages, with the teacher, with other adults, with visitors and with parents. This kind of working atmosphere cannot be achieved by a teacher working in isolation. The whole school has to work on these lines since such an enterprise involves the local community. The design of new schools reinforces this broadening approach to education, an approach which is not so much a revolution in mere methods as the evolution of certain principles and their outcomes in practice.

A teacher copes with the knowledge explosion, not by having a brainstorm as a result of straining to become a human (or inhuman) encyclopaedia, but by making knowledge accessible. Many primary schools have gone a long way towards solving the problems of the knowledge explosion as far as children learning and teachers teaching are concerned. Teachers are encouraged to have a specially developed interest and capability on which other members of staff in a team atmosphere can draw. Many people, creatures and objects share as allies in this undertaking. A visitor to a school of this kind occasionally feels that the children do not notice him, or at least do not appear to pay marked attention to the presence of a stranger because children are everywhere, because they are going about their business and because they are used to visitors. He may look round and have difficulty in finding the teacher. The good teacher in this situation is the unobtrusive one. Four-walled boxes and closed doors have largely disappeared. Instead there is, in some schools at any rate, one big learning space broken up into working areas. These areas are geared to a variety of activities: writing, painting, embroidery, cooking, mathematics, reading, construction and destruction. A child can get help from a teacher and it doesn't matter if it is his teacher or another one. There is a carpeted area for quiet bookish activities, with cushions, armchairs, a settee (and sometimes bunk beds) and different levels of floor, a place for coming together, for talk or for listening to a story. There are covered ways for noisy activities like woodwork and stonecutting. This is a positive, permissive, but controlled environment, a place of ordered freedom which rules out streaming, and rules out segregation by sex or ability or sometimes age. The classic example of such a social mix is the present-day survival of the all-age village school, to which, ironically, we have returned. At a seventeenth-century village in Yorkshire a visit was made to a one-teacher school of twenty-two children aged four to eleven. A four-year-old boy was sitting next to an eleven-year-old boy, and both were doing clay work, one helping the other in language he could understand, but both intent upon their work. The presence of the four-year-old in this particular instance was not holding the eleven-year-old back from producing an excellent piece of work, while the younger boy was being given some insights into the possibilities of clay.

A student of education can start to cope with the knowledge explosion by looking for the relevance of what he is doing in the classroom, and he will discover that teaching, in the sense of causing children to learn, gives a relevance to all the disciplines within education, to philosophy, to psychology and to sociology. For students about to become teachers it may be helpful to establish the following sequence of knowing: first of all knowing oneself, and knowing what really excites one as an all-absorbing interest, and how to pursue it, then knowing one's pupils and how to help them as individuals to seek the knowledge that is significant to them.

Apart from observing children's interests in action, during play or moments of leisure, watching their activities and listening to their talk, some knowledge of them may come to teachers through children's questions. Unfortunately some children's questions put to their teachers are not real ones, and are without any passionate concern to know the answer. Where the social climate is such that appreciation of a child's efforts can come from any quarter, not only from the teacher, and that genuine inquiry, sharing of experiences, respect for individuals and group activities are the order of the day, then questions will tend to demand answers leading to knowledge that does connect.

There is a danger that in some societies, including schools, where knowledge is identified with established truths, the emphasis will be upon the inculcation of facts by the most thorough, efficient, leaving-no-stone-unturned methods. Certain kinds of modern, technological devices, such as teaching machines and programmed learning, tended at one time to fit comfortably into this pattern until it was realized that in order to be in line with recent research into learning, greater efforts would have to be made to cater for the needs of individuals. The function of schools is to be places of encouragement rather than indoctrination, to encourage positive attitudes towards knowledge and to encourage individuals in their own peculiar pursuit of it.

Summary

Encouragement is the theme of this chapter, in which the ideas developed in the previous chapters are applied to the school. We examine the widespread tendency, among all age groups, adults and children alike, to stereotype their fellows and avoid the more demanding (yet more rewarding) task of valuing human beings for their uniqueness. The school can play an important part in reversing this tendency by cultivating a social climate of acceptance, catering for a wide variety of interests and choices and encouraging discussion and personal viewpoints. Individual projects are balanced with collaborative work in an environment in which personal relationships and communication are of vital importance. Basic skills are to be seen as necessary accomplishments in a meaningful context of individual, group and class work.

Teaching is best understood as an art, now increasingly supported by scientific method. Conditions for the exercise of this art are examined in a brief historical survey of the evolving classroom. Attention is given to two criteria in the evolution of classroom method: classroom organization and choice of learning material or content. In addition to a study of the development of general classroom organization, from the rigidity of the 1920s to the flexibility of today, two patterns of organization are examined separately: those related to the teaching of reading and mathematics respectively.

Factors affecting teachers' choice of learning content are then considered with motivation and nearness to children in mind. They include personal interests, topicality and environmental considerations, as well as work determined by the sequence of learning and even by accidental happenings. The chapter ends with some thoughts upon ways in which today's primary school teachers may cope with the knowledge explosion. It is to be hoped that ways may be found for schools to be places of encouragement for teachers as well as children, so they must not be burdened with having to 'know it all'. Co-operative teaching can come to their aid.

CHAPTER 6

CONCLUDING REMARKS

The term child-centred, applied to education, contains both obvious truth and misleading falsehood. Of course the learner is central in the event known as learning, but the importance of the teacher in this event has, as a result of this terminology, tended to be not only overlooked but sometimes even denied. In reaction against didacticism a generation of teachers has thought fit to apologize for being caught in the act of teaching. When I was about to be interviewed for a teaching post in the early 1950s, a well-meaning friend advised me: 'Whatever you do, don't tell them you like teaching. Say that you are interested in children learning.' For many who equated teaching with formal instruction, rows of desks and a blackboard, child-centredness meant leaving children to their own devices, free to follow short-lived interests, unguided and untutored. Without displacing children from the centre of the educational scene, certain studies in the last decade (Rosenshine 1971, Gage 1972, Dunkin and Biddle 1974, Dearden 1967, Richards 1973, Friedlander 1965, Eisner 1979) have served to reinstate the teacher as the *sine qua non* of the child's educational advancement. Some teachers may welcome this and the new austerity as an excuse to bring back outmoded methods of teaching, but too much has been learned in the first three-quarters of the twentieth century about child development and about ways in which children learn to halt progress by a return to an authoritarian past.

In the introduction to this book Peter was deliberately shown to be drawing. It might be thought that here is something a child can manage without the help of a teacher. Peter, like many children, enjoyed bringing into existence something that wasn't there before. Even without the intervention of his teacher he found himself being stimulated by something of which he was the maker. For this he did not need to conform to any external, adult standards. He was having the unique experience of creating his own standards from within. The fish which he created thus served an important educational function in the exercise of imagination, expression and judgement.

Then came Peter's teacher who, by interpreting his work, carried the educational process much further than Peter could have done without her help. She started by appreciating his efforts in specific terms, thus giving him confidence. She helped him towards independence of judgement by asking questions about his work, to which she expected reasoned answers. She expanded the expressive possibilities of his picture by constructive criticism, so that he was obliged to discover ways of making the visual content more convincing. She extended his speech vocabulary with a new word, but above all she drew from the child's own product educational meanings which gave the young artist a greater respect for his own work and a motive for persevering with it. The teacher was thus helping to clarify the child's thinking through the medium of his own expressive activity. Teacher and child were both totally involved. It is this kind of individualization of work which is the argument of this book. It means fluidity of approach and content, for there is no blueprint of method to be applied by all. Practice is the outcome of the sensitive understanding of children, of current ideas on education and the principles underlying them, and is unique to each situation and teacher.

Though the evolution of the primary school classroom, school architecture and furniture has facilitated the closer involvement of teachers with learners, not all teachers have felt comfortable with a more individual approach. In fact the survey of primary schools by H.M. Inspectors in 1978 showed that 75 percent of teachers preferred traditional methods. This is not a surprising finding, coming as it did after the William Tyndale inquiry which involved criticism, not only of one school, but also, in the minds of some authorities, implicated the whole recent philosophy of primary education. Considering how impossible a task it is to define a typical English primary school amid so much diversity, the idea of equating the William Tyndale approach with that of other schools was naturally felt by many primary school teachers to be an unjustifiable attack on their own work. Shipman (1975) ascribes the resistance to new methods to the apparent threat to the authority of the teacher by the unconventional use of space, blurring the roles of teacher and learner and undermining the idea of domination and subjection. The increased preparation needed, and the more exhausting nature of teaching where children were learning through activity, were further deterrents to innovation.

The fact that many teachers prefer to proceed cautiously does not imply a lack of understanding and care for children as individuals, though didactic class teaching does make it more difficult to give expression to this understanding and care. A greater degree of individualization of teaching approach and method is rendered more possible with smaller numbers in schools, flexible open-plan buildings, co-operative teaching, a curriculum offering wider choices and the disappearance of the examination at eleven-plus.

One of the results of the William Tyndale inquiry was an increased concern, on the part of government, about standards in education, and this was reflected in the Prime Minister's speech at Ruskin College, Oxford, in 1976. He emphasized that the goals of education were 'to equip children to the best of their ability for a lively, constructive place in society and also to fit them to do a job of work. . . . This means acquiring certain basic knowledge and skills and reasoning ability.' Unfair though it may be to remove sentences from their original context, such public statements have a familiar ring, echoing the pronouncements of earlier government spokesmen, and reminiscent of English elementary education with its emphasis on basic skills, a provision upon which 'depends our industrial prosperity' and 'also the good, the safe working of our constitutional system' (W.E. Forester introducing the 1870 Bill in the House of Commons, quoted in Maclure 1965)

Though primary school teachers resented the implied or imagined attack upon their own professional integrity, these events, leading to the call for a 'Great Debate', were not without their advantages. They have provided teachers with the opportunity to examine the whole question of standards, to define their aims and to realize the importance of their own confidence in themselves as professionals. Primary education in England and Wales is a direct descendant of the elementary school tradition, but it must be remembered that primary schools, as distinct from their ancestors, the elementary schools, have an honourable tradition of their own, none the less respectable for being of more recent origin. The best products of this younger tradition were to be seen in primary schools in the 1960s embodying the principles and recommendations of the Hadow Report of 1931. This report, published at a time of economic hardship, saw the primary school as a place of 'special opportunities, problems, and difficulties and these it must encounter by developing its own methods, perfecting its own technique and establishing more firmly its own standards of achievement and excellence. Its criterion must above all be the requirements of its pupils during the years when they are in its charge, not the exigencies of examinations or the demands of the schools and occupations which they will eventually enter. It will best serve their future by a single-minded devotion to their needs in the present, and the question which most concerns it is not what children should be – a point on which unanimity has hardly yet, perhaps, been reached – but what, in actual fact, children are. Its primary aim must be to aid children, while they are children, to be healthy and, so far as is possible, happy children, vigorous in body and lively in mind, in order that later, as with widening experience they grow toward maturity, the knowledge which life demands may more easily be mastered and the necessary accomplishments more readily acquired.'

It is in obedience to these principles that some of the best primary schools became forerunners of the new tradition established in the name of primary education. The facts of child nature and the observed characteristics of children of the particular age group were the recommended starting points of education. As a reminder to those who look for standards in primary education, the Hadow Report of 1931 deserves to be read and reread. If it be objected that times have changed since the 1930s, that is certainly true, but it must be remembered that this visionary, hopeful, yet realistic and practical report was compiled at a time of great social, industrial and international unrest. The rigours of the depression, mass unemployment and the threat of war were stark realities in the 1930s, yet the report establishes as its priorities, not the claims of a competing society, but the quality of life, the health and happiness of its children.

The report on the Primary School is quoted here as a reminder of a humanizing tradition originating from this report, and if there is to be a concern for the basics in education, thought needs to be given to the question of what the basics are. Efforts should be made by all those concerned with primary education to go forward in the primary school tradition, which was making good progress in the 1960s, rather than return for guidance to the older tradition of the elementary school with its narrow curriculum and limited objectives.

To be able to identify and describe standards involves a statement of the aims of education, calls in question the professionalism of teachers and has repercussions on teachers' self-confidence. Froebel referred to the teacher as a gardener and the children as plants. Many people have broken into this garden. As parents, administrators, providers of resources and taxpayers, they have rights of entry, but the teacher is still the gardener whose views on gardening deserve respect. Those who view the educational scene from outside tend to judge education in terms of measurable results. Their concern is with attainments that can be easily documented, especially those that provide access to a career. Parents cannot be blamed for desiring vocational security for their children, nor can employers for wanting an efficient workforce. Yet to listen exclusively to the voices of those who campaign for measurable results in education could lead to a narrowing of the curriculum, a reduction in the goals and expectations of teachers and in the ambitions of learners. Standards defined in oversimplified terms by those outside the teaching profession imply greater attention to measurable skills while ignoring the meaning of education itself. Even teachers are divided about the aims of education. As stated in the Schools Council Report of May 1975 (*The Aims of Primary Education*), there are those who consider the aim of education to be a preparation for life in a given society and those who give a stronger emphasis to individual values. There are some teachers who attach great importance to an end product while for others education is a never-ending process of growth. It is undeniable that much that is of value in education cannot be reduced to quantitative terms: the learner's awareness of himself and his own thoughts, his capacity to feel and to relate to others defy measurement. His sense of kinship with other human beings, his respect for their uniqueness, whether or not derived from his schooling, are part of his education and are of immense value to himself and to society, but difficult to submit to testing and documentation. His continuing curiosity about the universe and his lifelong interest in experiencing and learning are by their very nature too large to be contained in the examination results of the very school which stimulated them. The education of feeling, encouraged by the arts, and indeed by the sciences as well, together with imaginative and creative activities, are seldom included in the category of basic skills; yet it is important that these experiences, far from being decorative additions to the serious purposes of education, should be at the heart of the curriculum as a dynamic stimulus to learning. There is evidence that where the interests and imaginations of the young are engaged, competence in the basic skills appears to have benefited (*Primary*

Education in England, a survey by H.M. Inspectors of Schools, H.M.S.O. 1978). To encourage expressive activities is to expand language along with other skills, and with the arts as a motivator there is no fixed limit to standards. To have significance skills need to be incorporated in learning programmes which mirror the interdependence of human functions, the interaction of mind with body and feeling with intellect. This kind of emphasis in education involves a broad curriculum which takes account not only of measurable attainments but also of unquantifiable talents and interests. The above survey contains evidence that consideration for the interests and motivations of learners is not only a safeguard against alienation and underachievement at school but a stimulus for those very basic skills about which there is concern. It may be argued that a broad flexible programme is suitable for primary schools but not for secondary schools. Though this book is mainly concerned with junior and middle school education, I feel it is important that the same principles which support a broad curriculum are equally valid for all ages of learners.

When it comes to evaluating the results of a broadly based education, difficult though it is to express them in quantitative terms, they can nevertheless be expressed in descriptive language. It is surely not impossible to give guidance to pupils, parents and those interested in a child's education, in the form of a record of his attainments, interests and aptitudes, including folders of individual projects undertaken. These ideas are developed in detail for the secondary school in a book edited by Burgess and Adams (1980).

External-type examinations may no longer circumscribe the education of children in their middle years, yet educational progress has to be evaluated even for the satisfaction and guidance of the learner. It is a concern which needs to be removed from the arena of competition and set into the area of personal fulfilment. Because such evaluations involve greater understanding between teacher and pupil, they are closely linked with the idea of a system of education designed to meet the needs of individuals. These needs cannot be conceived in exclusively academic terms, as individual development must include progress in emotional maturity as well as in physical skills and expressiveness. It is measured (with some difficulty) in terms of social, moral and aesthetic awareness, as well as in the more accessible language of intellectual growth, literacy, numeracy and scientific knowledge. It involves not only the ability to think rationally, independently and without prejudice, but is also shown in examples of compassionate behaviour and kindness towards others.

Those who educate in an official capacity need to know whether or not their efforts are on the right lines. Progress needs to be recorded, if only for the encouragement of the learner, and to fulfil one of the most important purposes of education: to identify, uncover and foster talent. To be able to say that today's work is better than yesterday's, something more convincing is needed than a benign attitude. Progress has to be stated in specific terms if it is to carry any weight and persuasive power. There must be a dialogue involving parents as well, but the dialogue, as between Peter and his teacher, involves detailed appreciation and constructive criticism of the child's product, not generalities, as in some school reports. Peter's fish was bewildered-looking, and the picture needed to give a better suggestion of wateriness. The child's work was not just 'fair' or 'good' or 'showing promise'. In the act of reporting on Peter's work the teacher was still teaching, and this was teaching without directly instructing or indoctrinating. At other times instruction might have been the most expedient form for the teaching to take, but here she was merely eliciting, questioning, discussing, not even suggesting. This kind of teaching is noninterfering in the Froebelian sense. The point is that, however discreet and inconspicuous the teaching, the teacher is absolutely vital to the child's progress. Peter was learning new attitudes and a new vocabulary as well as how to draw.

Though pupils in the middle years of schooling are not under the same pressures of external examinations as those who are about to leave school, there are a number of ways in which their progress can be recorded, taking into account both the broader personal aspects of development as well as the academic and basic educational objectives. Conversations with children, cumulative records, communal projects involving shared tasks, children's own diaries and reports of personal experience, self-appraisals, statements or folders of individual interests and choices in the fields of learning and leisure are possible suggestions for approaching rather than covering the vast spectrum of educational aims, so many of which, for example, intellectual autonomy, sensitivity, creativity and moral development, cannot be measured. Communication with parents can also help to give a clearer picture of a child's achievements, for all concerned (Downey and Kelly 1979). Inevitably such an approach means extra work for the teacher, but it would have compensations in a greater knowledge of his pupils as people.

Evaluations of progress would not be a once-and-for-all report, but a continuous process to which the child contributes in discussion and self-evaluation.

The undeniable fact of human differences has gradually led to the abandonment of mass teaching in schools which cater for individual abilities and interests. The same fact is producing similar reactions to the practice of evaluating the results of education according to a common yardstick (Burgess and Adams 1980).

The criterion of comparability begins to disappear from a descriptive assessment as the idea of competition disappears from an individualized curriculum. Though examinations will no doubt continue as employers and institutions, such as universities, continue to demand minimum qualifications for employment and for entrance based on comparisons between one candidate and another, a descriptive record might eventually prove a more reliable index of suitability for a career than the traditional once-and-for-all pass/fail categories. The element of competition receives little or no emphasis in an individualized approach, but paradoxically, collaboration in joint enterprises is no contradiction to such a programme, encouraging as it does the varied talents of individuals.

Because the ultimate responsibility for the quality of education rests with the teacher it is essential that teachers as professionals should trust their own judgement and have confidence in themselves. Their understanding of education, and their awareness that it is of value in itself, provide the basis for this confidence. Such assurance requires sound teacher education and strong support for young teachers during their first years of service. It is important, too, that teachers, like the pupils whom they teach, continue to study and be ever curious and willing to learn. They need to be self-critical and able to adapt to change. They need encouragement, too, through the provision of resources and the free exchange of ideas. This implies that there should be well-organized and open channels of communication between all who are concerned with education, including parents and administrators, and between the teachers themselves within and across the age groups they teach. Some schools do take the trouble to explain their philosophy, aims and methods to parents, in the hope that, on a basis of mutual understanding, parents can feel more able to participate in the activities and purposes of the school.

Where communication with parents leads to mutual understanding and cooperation, not only does the school receive support for its values, but children are more likely to make progress in their education (Plowden 1967, Shipman 1975).

The purpose of education as defined in the Hadow Report (1931) was expressed as follows: 'What a wise and good parent will desire for his own children a nation must desire for all children.' Wise and good parents think of their children as unique. It is unlikely, therefore, that they would complain about a school because its teachers made it clear that they were trying to treat their children according to the same standpoint.

Summary

The concluding remarks contained in this chapter emphasize again the importance of the teacher in the education of children. Amid the clamour of voices raised in discussions about standards in education, that of the teacher, as a professional, deserves to be heard. There is the danger that, in giving way to a popular insistence upon standards defined in simplistic terms, teachers, by paying too much attention to those aspects of education that can be tested, will tend to overlook some of the broader human vistas of education represented, for example, by the arts and sciences, by environmental explorations and other activities, the outcomes of which are difficult to measure. This would amount to no less than a betrayal of the primary school tradition, originating from the Hadow Report of 1931, in favour of the earlier elementary school tradition with its narrow curriculum and minimal requirements.

It is essential, therefore, that through sound teacher education teachers understand the value of education for its own sake, and have confidence, as professionals, in themselves and in their work, and their own ideas about aims and standards based upon this understanding.

Concern for basic skills requires an integrated programme which provides a context for them, and does not imply a neglect of those creative activities which stimulate and motivate learning. A child's progress in broadly based work may not be measurable in quantitative terms, but it is not impossible to devise records of progress written in English prose.

Where comparability and competition assume less importance in individualized schemes of work, it is essential that schools communicate their ideas freely to parents and to all who are concerned in the education of children.

REFERENCES

Argyle, M., (1967), *The Psychology of Interpersonal Behaviour*, Penguin.
Ashton, P., Kneen, P., Davies, F. and Holley, B.J., (1975), *The Aims of Primary Education: A study of teachers' opinions*, Macmillan.
Ausubel, D.P., (1969), *School Learning*, Rinehart and Winston.
Banks, O., (1968), *The Sociology of Education*, Batsford.
Barnes, D., (1976), *From Communication to Curriculum*, Penguin.
Bennett, N., (1976), *Teaching Styles and Pupil Progress*, Open Books.
Bennet, N. and McNamara, D., (1979), *Focus on Teaching, Readings in the observation and conceptualisation of teaching*, Longman.
Berliner, D.C., (1976), 'Impediments to the study of teacher effectiveness', in Bennett, N. and McNamara D., op. cit
Bernstein, B., (1972), 'Education cannot compensate for society', in Cashdan, S., (ed.), *Language in Education*, Routledge & Kegan Paul with Oxford University Press.
Brown, G., Cherrington, D.H. and Cohen, L., (1975), *Experiments in the Social Sciences*, Harper & Row.
Bruner, J., (1960), *The Process of Education*, New York, Vintage Books.
Bruner, J., (1966), *Studies in Cognitive Growth*, Wiley.
Bruner, J., (1972), 'The relevance of skill, or the skill of relevance', in Bruner, J.S., *The Relevance of Education*, Allen and Unwin.
Burgess, T. and Adams, E., (eds.), (1980), *Outcomes of Education*, Macmillan.
Central Advisory Council for Education, (1967), *Children and Their Primary Schools*, (Plowden Report), H.M.S.O.

Choat, E., (1978), *Children's Acquisition of Mathematics*, N.F.E.R. Publishing Company.

Choat, E., (1980), *Mathematics and the Primary School Curriculum*, N.F.E.R. Publishing Company.

Consultative Committee on the Primary School (1931), Report of the Consultative Committee on the Primary School (Hadow), H.M.S.O.

Daniel, M.V., (1947), *Activity in the Primary School*, Blackwell.

Dearden, R.F., (1967), 'Instruction and learning by discovery', in Peters R.S., (ed.), *The Concept of Education*, Routledge & Kegan Paul.

Dewey, J. (1916) Democracy and Education, Macmillan.

Donaldson, M. (1978) Children's Minds, Fontana/Collins.

Douglas, J. W. B., (1964), *The Home and the School*, McGibbon and Kee.

Downey, M.E. and Kelly, A.V., (1979), *Theory and Practice of Education*, Harper & Row, second edition.

Downey, M.E., (1977), *Interpersonal Judgements in Education*, Harper & Row.

Dunkin, M.J. and Biddle, B.J., (1974), *The Study of Teaching*, Holt, Rinehart and Winston.

Eisner, E.W., (1979), 'The contribution of painting to children's cognitive development', *Journal of Curriculum Studies*, 1979, Vol. II, No. 2.

Erikson, E.H. (1951) Childhood and Society. New York, Norton. Penguin, 1965.

Flanders, N.A. and Simon, A., (1969), 'Teacher effectiveness', in Ebel, A.L., (ed.), *Encyclopedia of Educational Research*.

Friedlander, B.Z., (1965), 'A psychologist's second thoughts on concepts, curiosity and discovery in teaching and learning', *Harvard Educational Review*, Vol. 35, No. 1.

Froebel, F., (1887), *The Education of Man*, (translated from the German and annotated by W. N. Hailmann), New York, D. Appleton and Co.

Gage, N. L., (1972), *Teacher Effectiveness and Teacher Education*, Pacific Palo Alto.

Galton, M., Simon, B., and Croll, P., (1980), (Oracle), *Inside the Primary Classroom*, Routledge & Kegan Paul.

Gesell, A. and Ilg, F.L., (1946), *The Child from 5 to 10*, New York, Harper & Row.

Goldman, R.J., (1965), *Readiness for Religion: a basis for developmental religious education*, Routledge & Kegan Paul.

Hamilton, D. and Delamont, S., (1974), 'Classroom research: a cautionary tale', in Bennett, N. and McNamara, D., op cit.

Hirst, P.H. and Peters, R.S., (1970), *The Logic of Education*, Routledge & Kegan Paul.

Hogben, D., (1972), 'The behavioural objectives approach: Some problems and some dangers', *Journal of Curriculum Studies*, Vol. 4, No. 1.

Holmes, E., (1911), *What Is and What Might Be*, Constable.

Holt, J., (1964), *How Children Fail*, Penguin.

Howard, L., (1952), *Birds as Individuals*, Collins.

Hughes, M. (1975) Egocentrism in pre-school children, Edinburgh University unpublished doctoral dissertation, referred to in Donaldson (1978).

Hunt, J. McV., (1971), 'Using intrinsic motivation to teach young children', reprinted in Cashdan, A. and Whitehead, D., (eds.), *Personality Theory and Learning*, Routledge & Kegan Paul.

Huxley, A., (1963), *Literature and Science*, Chatto and Windus.

Isaacs, S. (1930) Intellectual Growth in Young Children, Routledge & Kegan Paul.

Isaacs, S. (1933) Social Development in Young Children, George Routledge and Sons Ltd.

Jarman, C., (1972), *Display and Presentation in Schools*, A. & C. Black.

Jones, R.M., (1972), *Fantasy and Feeling in Education*, Penguin.

Jung, C., (1958), *The Undiscovered Self*, Routledge & Kegan Paul.

Kohlberg, L., (1966), 'Moral Education in the Schools', *School Review*.

Little, A. and Westergaard, J., (1964), 'The trend of class differentials in educational opportunity in England and Wales', *British Journal of Sociology*, Vol. 15.

Maclure, J Stuart, (ed.), (1965), *Educational Documents in England and Wales: 1816 to the present day*, Methuen.

Marshall, S., (1963), *An Experiment in Education*, Cambridge University Press.

McClelland, D.C. et al., (1953), *The Achievement Motive*, Appleton-Century Crofts.

McNamara, D. and Desforges, C., (1978), 'The social sciences, teacher education and the objectification of craft knowledge', in Bennett, N. and McNamara, D., op cit.

Midwinter, E., (1972), *Priority Education*, Penguin.

Opie, I. and P., (1959), *The Language and Lore of Schoolchildren*, Oxford University Press.

Peters, R.S., (1966), *Ethics and Education*, Allen and Unwin.

Piaget, J., (1929), *The Child's Conception of the World*, Routledge & Kegan Paul.

Piaget, J., (1950), *The Psychology of Intelligence*, Harcourt Brace.

Piaget, J., (1952a) *The Child's Conception of Number*, Routledge & Kegan Paul.

Piaget, J., (1952b), *The Origins of Intelligence in Children*, International Universities Press.

Piaget, J., and Inhelder, B. (1956), *The Child's Conception of Space*, Routledge & Kegan Paul.

Pluckrose, H., (1979), *Children in their Primary Schools*, Penguin and Harper & Row.

Primary Education in England, a Survey by H.M. Inspectors of Schools (1978), H.M.S.O.

Raban, B., Wells, G., and Nash, T., (1976), 'Observing children learning to read' in Bennett, N. and McNamara, D., op cit.

Richards, C., (1973), 'Third thoughts on discovery', *Educational Review*, Vol. 25, No. 2.

Richardson, M., (1935), *Writing and Writing Patterns*, University of London Press.

Rosen, C. and H., (1973), 'The language of primary school children', chapter 2, *Talking*, Penguin.

Rosenshine, B., (1971), *Teaching Behaviours and Student Achievement*, National Foundation for Educational Research.

Shipman, M.D., (1975), *The Sociology of the School*, Longman.

Sinclair de Zwart, H., (1969), 'Developmental psycholinguistics', in Elkind, D., and Flavell, J., *Studies in Cognitive Development*, Oxford University Press.

Stone, A.L., (1949), *Story of a School*, Ministry of Education Pamphlet No. 14, H.M.S.O.

Stubbs, M., (1976), *Language, Schools and Classrooms*, Methuen.

Taylor Report (1977), A New Partnership for our Schools, H.M.S.O.

Tough, J., (1973), *Focus on Meaning*, Allen and Unwin.

Tough, J., (1977), *The Development of Meaning*, Allen and Unwin.

Washburne, C., (1932), *Adjusting the School to the Child*, New York, World Book Co.

Wheatley, D., (1977), 'Mathematical concepts and language', in *New Era and Ideas*, Vol. 58, No. 5, 1977.

Whitehead, A.N., (1932), *Aims of Education*, Williams and Norgate.
Wilson, P.S., (1971), *Interest and Discipline in Education*, Routledge & Kegan Paul.

Additional reading:

Gammage, P., (1971), *Teacher and Pupil*, Routledge & Kegan Paul.
Marsh, L., (1970), *Alongside the Child*, A.& C. Black.
Marsh, L., (1973), *Being a Teacher*, A. & C. Black.
Read, H., (1956), *Education Through Art*, Pantheon Books.

Author Index

Adams, E., 47, 133, 135, 137
Argyle, M., 6, 137
Ashton, P., 82, 137
Ausubel, D.P., 45, 137

Banks, O., 22, 137
Barnes, D., 15, 20, 137
Bennett, N., 30, 31, 137, 139, 140
Berliner, D.C., 31, 137
Bernstein, B., 22, 137
Biddle, B.J., 32, 128, 138
Brontes, 8
Brown, G., 76, 137
Bruner, J., 16, 25, 46, 123, 137
Burgess, T., 47, 133, 135, 137

Cashdan, A., 61, 139
Cashdan, S., 22, 137
Central Advisory Council for Education, 1, 4, 7, 22, 54, 56, 122, 136, 137
Cherrington, D.H., 76, 137
Choat, E., 26, 31, 138
Cohen, L., 76, 137
Consultative Committee on the Primary School, 8, 20, 21, 49, 77, 121, 122, 130, 131, 136, 138
Croll, P., 30, 31, 90, 138

Daniel, M.V., 20, 138
Davies, F., 82, 137
Dearden, R.F., 45, 128, 138
Delamont, S., 31, 139
Desforges, C., 32, 139
Dewey, J., 7, 138
Dickens, C., 7
Donaldson, M., 53, 138
Douglas, J.W.B., 22, 138
Downey, M.E., 6, 10, 13, 38, 134, 138
Dunkin, M.J., 32, 128, 138

Ebel, A.L., 32, 138
Eisner, E.W., 31, 94, 128, 138
Elkind, D., 19, 140
Erikson, E.H., 16, 138

Flanders, N.A., 32, 138
Flavell, J., 19, 140
Freud, S., 16, 58
Friedlander, B.Z., 46, 128, 138
Froebel, F., 7, 41, 51, 93, 94, 132, 134, 138

Gage, N.L., 32, 128, 138
Galton, M., 30, 31, 90, 138
Gammage, P., 141
Gesell, A., 57, 138

Goldman, R.J., 138

Hadow, 8, 20,, 21, 49, 77, 121, 122, 130, 131, 136, 138
Hamilton, D., 31, 139
Her Majesty's Inspectors, 30, 129, 133, 140
Hirst, P.H., 13, 122, 139
Hogben, D., 15, 139
Holley, B.J., 82, 137
Holmes, E., 7, 139
Holt, J., 51, 139
Howard, L. 49, 139
Hughes, M., 53, 139
Hunt, J., McV., 61, 139
Huxley, A., 88, 139

Ilg, F.L., 57, 138
Inhelder, 110, 139
Isaacs, S., 93, 139

Jarman, C., 24, 139
Jones, R.M., 19, 139
Jung, C., 35, 139

Kelly, A.V., 6, 10, 134, 138
Kneen, P., 82, 137
Kohlberg, L., 81, 139

Little, A., 22, 38, 139
Locke, J., 18

Maclure, J.S., 130, 139
Marsh, L., 141
Marshall, S., 19, 21, 139
McClelland, D.C., 60, 139
McMillan, M., 93
McMillan, R., 93
McNamara, D., 32, 137, 139, 140
Midwinter, E., 20, 139
Montessori, M., 7, 60, 93

Nash, T., 31, 140
National Foundation for Educational Research, 26
Neill, A.S., 7
New Education Fellowship, 7

Opie, I. and P., 102, 139
Oracle, 30, 31, 90, 138

Pestalozzi, 7
Peters, R.S., 12, 13, 139, 140
Piaget, J., 16, 18, 26, 31, 35, 52, 53, 58, 68, 81, 110, 114, 124, 140
Plato, 7
Plowden, 1, 4, 7, 22, 54, 56, 122, 136, 137
Pluckrose, H., 115, 140
Raban, B., 31, 140
Read, H., 141
Richards, C., 45, 46, 128, 140
Richardson, M., 94, 140
Rosen, C. and H., 64, 140
Rosenshine, B., 32, 128, 140
Rousseau, J.J., 7, 40

Shipman, M.D., 2, 115, 129, 136, 140
Simon, A., 32, 138
Simon, B., 30, 31, 90, 138
Sinclair de Zwart, H., 19, 140
Stone, A.L., 19, 140
Stubbs, M., 15, 20, 85, 140

Taylor Report, 82, 100, 140
Tough, J., 25, 64, 140

Washburne, C., 37, 140
Wells, G., 31, 140
Westergaard, J., 22, 38, 139
Wheatley, D., 26, 140
Whitehead, A.N., 124, 141
Whitehead, D., 61, 139
Wilson, P.S., 109, 141

Subject Index

ability, 11, 16, 19, 23, 38, 40, 42, 48, 50, 80, 84, 86, 91, 95, 101, 102, 103, 110, 112, 122, 124, 125, 133, 135

acceptance, 5, 13, 37, 58, 59, 64, 65, 77, 80, 81, 86, 90, 127

accidental topics, 109, 119, 127

accommodation, 18, 57

accountability, 47

achievement, 12, 22, 26, 30, 31, 38, 43, 58, 60-65, 66, 69, 76, 77, 78, 80, 84, 86, 98, 104, 107, 134

acquisitiveness, 60, 74-76, 80

activity, 5, 7, 20, 21, 24, 25, 26, 30, 31, 38, 43, 45, 46, 56, 60, 66, 67-74, 68, 75, 76, 77, 78, 79, 80, 84, 86, 87, 88, 91, 94, 97, 100, 105, 106, 107, 114, 121, 122, 123, 126, 130

administration, 7, 19, 33, 46, 47, 55, 132, 135

adolescence, 8, 54, 55, 58, 63, 67, 68, 77

adventure, 24, 58, 68, 69, 70, 71, 77, 98, 120

advisers, 10, 93

aesthetic awareness, 133

aims, 38, 45, 46, 82, 104, 105, 108, 130, 131, 132, 134, 135, 136

alienation, 2, 133

alternative ways of living, 10

appreciation, 61, 126, 129, 134

aptitudes, 133

archaeology, 67, 111, 112

architecture, 76, 100, 101, 110

art, 19, 21, 23, 31, 32, 34, 37, 42, 43, 58, 62, 66, 86, 87, 88, 89, 90, 94, 96, 99, 106, 109, 111, 117, 120, 122, 125, 127, 132, 136

assessments, 59, 135

assessment of performance unit, 30, 47

assimilation, 18

attainment, 11, 26, 40, 84, 103, 132, 133

attention, 23, 25, 31, 44, 87, 106, 110

attitudes of teachers, 2, 3, 6, 13, 39, 49, 98

audio-visual equipment, 39

authority, 9, 13, 15, 16, 22, 40, 49, 63, 76, 98, 129

backwardness, 22, 74, 78, 86, 97, 103, 118, 123

behaviourists, 58

book reviews, 104, 105

books, 4, 16, 43, 47, 62, 63, 71, 72, 79, 86, 88, 97, 98, 101, 103, 104, 105, 109, 115, 119, 121, 122, 124 building design, 17, 18, 26, 55, 125, 129

changes in primary schools, 11-34
characteristics of the middle years, 60-80
child-centred education, 8, 17, 42, 98, 128
child development, 6, 13, 18, 21, 26, 35, 38, 48, 53, 54, 55, 58, 59, 64, 69, 78, 79, 86, 89, 128
child study, 38, 49, 57, 89, 93, 94, 98
choice of learning material, 91, 107-126, 127
choices, 10, 12, 17, 20, 21, 25, 34, 38, 40, 42, 43, 47, 50, 61, 85, 86, 94, 95, 97, 98, 100, 104, 112, 124, 127, 130, 134.
classroom furniture, 12, 18, 47, 92, 97, 129
classroom incidents, 2-5, 14-16, 33, 51
classroom organization, 16, 33, 50, 87, 91-107, 108, 127
class teaching, 4, 21, 38, 90, 95, 99, 100, 101, 102
class work, 47, 97, 100, 127
clinical procedures, 35, 57
cognitive development, 16, 19, 25, 31, 52, 58
collaboration, 17, 135
collections, 22, 43, 66, 74, 75, 107, 111, 115
common core curriculum, 82, 107
communication, 8, 26, 31, 37, 45, 59, 64, 66, 76, 79, 88, 89, 91, 99, 102, 122, 127, 134, 135, 136
community, 19, 33, 37, 40, 41, 43, 76, 81, 82, 83, 85, 100, 108, 114, 121, 123, 125
community education, 20
community school, 19-20
comparability, 47, 135, 136

compensatory education, 22, 24
competition, 3, 64, 81, 133, 135, 136
comprehension, 102, 103, 104, 105
concepts, 18, 25, 26-30, 35, 52, 75, 76, 81, 102, 110
concrete operations, 52, 58
conversation, 20, 24, 25, 39, 42, 51, 63, 64, 68, 70, 78, 107, 134
cooking, 43, 84, 86, 125
co-operation, 41, 43, 86, 89, 135
co-operative teaching, 34, 101, 127, 130
craft, 37, 42, 43, 66, 84, 90, 96, 122, 125
creative writing, 102
creativity, 23, 32, 45, 54, 69, 89, 99, 120, 134
cross-sectional studies, 48, 57
cumulative records, 134
curiosity, 21, 44, 45, 46, 58, 68, 69, 77, 85, 98, 102, 104, 109, 114, 132, 135
curriculum, 18, 21, 30, 36, 77, 81, 82, 84, 85, 94, 95, 102, 105, 107, 110, 121, 122, 130, 131, 132, 133, 136

Dance, 19, 37, 86
delinquency, 21
democracy, 7, 9, 13, 19, 81
deprivation, 24, 25, 59
Deptford, 2, 73, 93, 115
depth psychology, 58
desire to learn, 60, 65-67, 80, 99
discipline, 110
discovery, 21, 44, 45, 46, 58, 66, 77, 99, 112, 114, 121
discussion, 13, 15, 16, 23, 31, 37, 41, 42, 43, 69, 70, 86, 94, 96, 99, 101, 102, 105, 112, 120, 124, 127, 134, 135
display, 23, 95, 113
distance, 3, 33, 40, 41, 91, 92, 96, 108
diversity, 7, 32, 33, 35, 47, 84, 85, 86,

100, 101, 106, 108, 129
dogma, 42, 44
drama, 19, 21, 43, 72, 73, 74, 75, 86, 91, 105, 111, 117
dramatic play, 22, 72, 73, 74

educational priority areas, 20, 22
egocentrism, 52, 53, 64, 65, 67
elementary school, 7, 8, 108, 130, 131, 136
Emile, 7, 40
emotional development, 31, 94, 96, 133
empathy, 37, 69, 94
encouragement, 1, 12, 17, 20, 32, 38, 43, 46, 59, 81, 85, 86, 97, 98, 103, 112, 121, 124, 126, 127, 134, 135
environment, 7, 10, 11, 21-25, 31, 32, 33, 34, 40, 41, 42, 46, 48, 49, 54, 56, 59, 60, 65, 66, 67, 68, 69, 76, 77, 90, 91, 93, 96, 97, 99, 100, 110, 111, 113, 114, 115, 125, 127, 136
environmental studies, 22, 37, 66, 67, 101, 109, 111, 124
equality, 9, 76
Essex Tests, 26-30
evaluation, 31, 61, 96, 103, 133, 135
examinations, 3, 47, 82, 108, 123, 124, 130, 131, 132, 134, 135
excursions, 65, 67, 100, 101, 109, 111, 112, 115
expectations, 38, 43, 56, 58, 69, 83, 86, 132
experience, 5, 11, 13, 18-21, 22, 24, 25, 26, 31, 32, 33, 34, 37, 38, 40, 43, 47, 50, 52, 56, 62, 63, 66, 69, 73, 76, 77, 81, 85, 88, 91, 101, 102, 109, 111, 112, 113, 114, 117, 118, 121, 122, 124, 126, 134
experiment, 7, 12, 13, 21, 22, 58, 59, 66, 69, 76, 88, 90, 96, 98, 101, 105, 107, 109, 110, 120

experimental techniques, 57
exploration, 22, 45, 60, 65, 66, 68, 69, 74, 77, 109, 121, 136
exploratory thinking, 15
expressive arts, 19, 34, 96, 122, 129, 132, 133, 136

family, 24, 41, 43, 55, 56, 63, 64, 74, 77
family grouping, 19, 26, 101
fantasy, 24, 62, 65, 67, 71
field studies, 22
film, 8, 24, 39, 47, 50, 66
first school, 56, 57, 70, 94
flexibility, 16, 18, 34, 39, 45, 56, 77, 86, 97-99, 101, 107, 127
formal operations, 53, 58
freedom, 7, 12, 13, 16, 21, 42, 45, 61, 60, 81, 82, 88, 90, 93, 94, 99, 100
friendships, 19, 99
Froebel movement, 93
furniture, 12, 18, 47, 92, 97, 129

gardening, 66, 75
geography, 41, 46, 71, 95, 106, 111
geometry, 42, 110
grammar, 51, 102
Great Debate, 82, 130
groupings, 16, 19, 26, 89, 95, 98, 99-101, 105, 108
groups, 3, 35, 36, 37, 38, 39, 40, 41, 42, 43, 47, 48, 55, 57, 58, 59, 60, 63, 65, 69, 71, 72, 73, 76, 77, 79, 80, 81, 83, 84, 87, 89, 90, 91, 92, 95, 96, 97, 98, 103, 106, 107, 112, 127
group work, 21, 34, 50, 55, 87, 90, 96, 97, 100, 101, 105, 106, 126, 127

handicapped children, 12, 86, 93, 108, 114, 123, 124
handwriting, 62, 94, 106
heredity, 33, 56

high schools, 56
history, 12, 14, 15, 16, 41, 46, 75, 76,
    95, 97, 106, 107, 111, 123
human development, 52, 53, 57, 58,
    59
human rights, 76

identity, 9, 33, 58, 72, 77, 98
imagination, 21, 22, 24, 53, 60, 62, 67,
    68, 72, 73, 79, 80, 89, 102, 120, 129,
    132
incentive, 61
individual attention, 1, 16
individual differences, 11, 16-18, 32,
    33, 39, 48, 49, 57, 59, 60, 76, 80, 81,
    83, 84, 87, 112, 135
individualized work, 18, 26, 33, 35,
    36, 37, 38, 39, 43, 47, 50, 56, 57, 80,
    81, 87, 90, 95, 97, 100, 124, 129,
    130, 136
individual work, 21, 34, 40, 50, 55, 90,
    97, 100, 107, 124, 127, 133
indoctrination, 16, 21, 126
infancy, 58
infants, 56, 60, 65, 93, 94, 95
infant schools, 37, 56, 57, 70, 94, 95,
    105
innercity, 2, 89, 96, 115
innovation, 20, 98, 130
inquiry, 8, 9, 13, 17, 49, 65, 66, 71, 85,
    126, 129, 130
instruction, 9, 32, 44, 52, 91, 92, 108,
    128, 134
integrated day, 32, 95, 96, 97
intellectual development, 16, 19, 23,
    25, 31, 41, 44, 55, 86, 93, 94, 96,
    133
interaction analysis, 32
interests, 11, 12, 13, 15, 16, 17, 18, 21,
    23, 25, 31, 34, 38, 39, 40, 41, 42, 43,
    44, 46, 50, 58, 59, 60, 70, 74, 75, 77,
    80, 81, 82, 83, 85, 86, 87, 96, 97, 99,

100, 101, 104, 107, 108, 109, 112,
    113, 117, 118, 121, 126, 127, 128,
    132, 133, 134, 135
inter-related learning, 17, 22
intuitive stage, 52
investigation, 7, 13, 15, 20, 22, 23, 45,
    52, 68, 69, 107, 112, 119
Isle of Dogs, 2

junior children, 1, 12, 13, 41, 56, 58,
    60, 63, 65, 67, 69, 72, 74, 80, 84,
    101, 102, 118, 124
junior school, 1, 8, 55, 56, 57, 62, 67,
    95, 105, 106, 107, 111, 133

kindergarten, 93
knowledge, 9, 13, 17, 24, 30, 37, 38,
    42, 45, 46, 49, 63, 65, 66, 76, 77, 89,
    109, 120-127, 130

laissez-faire, 13
language, 5, 22, 23, 25, 26-30, 32, 37,
    45, 52, 58, 64, 65, 73, 74, 79, 91, 96,
    99, 101, 102, 106
language laboratories, 39, 107, 110,
    133
language master, 39
learning, 9-12, 17, 18-21, 31, 32,
    34-38, 40, 41, 42, 45-48, 51, 52, 54,
    56, 57, 58, 65-67, 68, 69, 76, 77, 79,
    80, 81, 86-92, 94, 97-103, 108, 111,
    114, 119, 120, 123, 124, 125, 126,
    128, 130, 132, 133, 134, 135, 136
leisure, 10, 73, 77, 123, 126, 134
libraries, 15, 20, 96, 103, 104, 109, 112
listening, 12, 15, 16, 20, 21, 25, 37, 43,
    44, 45, 54, 61, 63, 71, 84, 89, 114,
    126
literacy, 109, 133
literature, 19, 21, 31, 43, 97, 104
local education authority, 82
longitudinal studies, 43, 57

make-believe, 70-74

mass media, 8, 16, 22, 24, 66, 122

materials, 12, 16, 17, 18, 22, 23, 38, 39, 40, 47, 61, 74, 88, 94, 98, 101, 114, 119, 124

mathematics, 21, 24, 26-30, 31, 32, 37, 41, 42, 47, 52, 62, 78, 79, 81, 95, 96, 101, 106, 107, 108, 110, 118, 123, 125, 127

methods, 16, 18, 30, 36, 37, 67, 92, 93, 98, 99, 100, 125, 128, 129, 130, 131, 135

middle school, 1, 7, 12, 55, 56, 57, 60, 62, 67, 69, 80, 107, 133

middle years, 1, 48, 50, 54-59, 60-80, 133, 134

mixed ability, 51, 97

mobility, 8, 17, 58, 92-94

moral development, 71, 113, 114

morality, 31, 76, 81

moral values, 31, 52, 76, 115

motivation, 2, 13, 44, 45, 53, 54, 60, 68, 78, 89, 96, 121, 122, 124, 127, 129, 133, 136

movement, 19, 21, 52, 61, 66, 69, 73, 86, 96, 111

multi-cultural classroom, 84, 99, 117

museums, 66, 75, 100, 109, 111

music, 19, 21, 37, 44, 66, 100, 102, 106, 109, 110, 111, 117

National Child Development Study, 57

nearness, 35, 40, 41, 91, 98, 111, 127

neighbourhood projects, 67, 100

New Education Fellowship, 7

non-streaming, 19

number, 81, 100, 110

numeracy, 109, 133

nursery school, 56, 93

objectives, 15, 38, 45, 104, 131, 134

observation, 12, 16, 21, 23, 30, 31, 39, 40, 41, 42, 43, 46, 48, 49, 50, 52, 54, 57, 58, 60, 61, 70, 73, 76, 78, 93, 94, 102, 105, 111, 114, 119, 124

open plan schools, 17, 32, 34, 97, 130

open society, 9

oracle study, 30, 31, 57, 90

order, 98, 124, 125

organization, 16, 17, 18, 33, 36, 43, 48, 82, 87, 90, 91-107, 108, 111, 127

overhead projector, 39

parents, 2, 9, 10, 16, 19, 36, 49, 57, 59, 49, 70, 82, 86, 96, 100, 113, 125, 132, 133, 134, 135, 136

payment by results, 4

personality, 5, 11, 16, 39, 43, 79, 83, 84

personal topics, 109, 117

philosophy, 1, 2, 3, 18, 86, 99, 109, 126, 129, 135

physical education, 19, 32, 37, 41, 66, 69, 79, 98, 106, 109

pioneers, 93, 94, 105

play, 31, 61, 62, 67, 72, 73, 74, 75, 77, 83, 99, 124, 126

play centre, 62, 73, 84, 124

Plowden Committee and Report, 1, 4, 7, 22, 55, 56, 122, 136

pluralist society, 9, 76

poetry, 21, 37, 102, 113, 115, 116, 117, 122

practice, 1, 6, 10, 12, 21, 30, 35, 38, 39, 45, 49, 53, 54, 78, 103, 125, 129

pre-school, 55, 67, 93

primary education, 1, 4, 6-34, 42, 46, 82, 90, 108, 109, 130, 131

primary education survey, 30, 129, 133, 140

primary school, 1, 2, 7, 8, 10, 11, 19, 21, 25, 30, 31, 32, 33, 37, 40, 41, 46, 55, 58, 66, 67, 69, 76, 81, 84, 85, 87,

89, 90, 92, 96, 100, 102, 108, 109,
111, 115, 121, 122, 123, 125, 127,
129, 130, 131, 133, 136
priority areas, 20, 22
problems, 1, 7, 13, 16, 30, 33, 35, 41,
50, 53, 65, 77, 84, 85, 101, 106, 121
programmed learning, 126
progress, 6, 7, 18, 30, 33, 59, 62, 80,
81, 89, 93, 95, 96, 103, 130, 133,
134, 135, 136
projects, 2, 11, 12, 37, 43, 47, 50, 62,
67, 95, 111, 112, 124, 127, 133, 134
provision, 16, 17, 18, 22, 45, 46, 50,
55, 56, 57, 59, 68, 98, 104, 114, 121,
135
pseudo-dialogue, 15, 85
psychology, 16, 18, 35, 44, 48, 49, 53,
55, 58, 64, 67, 69, 81, 88, 89, 93, 98,
99, 109, 114, 126
puberty, 58

questions, 3, 4, 15, 20, 35, 37, 38, 51,
52, 54, 65, 66, 69, 74, 85, 92, 103,
104, 105, 107, 109, 123, 126, 129,
134

radio, 8, 9. 65
reading, 11, 17, 23, 31, 41, 54, 62, 69,
71, 72, 77, 78, 79, 86, 95, 96, 97,
101-106, 108, 110, 125, 127
records, 18, 95, 103, 133, 134, 135,
136
reformers, 7, 10
relationships, 2, 4, 5, 6, 9, 12, 17, 19,
23, 31, 32, 33, 34, 36, 40, 43, 45, 46,
48, 52, 54, 56, 88, 89, 90, 94, 98,
101, 114, 122, 124, 127
religion, 9, 58, 114, 117
reporting, 37, 134, 135
research, 2, 10, 18, 22, 30, 31, 32, 35,
46, 48, 52, 53, 54, 55, 58, 67, 81, 87,
88, 89, 105, 110, 114, 126

resources, 22, 26, 34, 36, 38, 39, 43,
46, 57, 66, 81, 89, 95, 97, 100, 101,
104, 114, 121, 124, 135
respect for children, 11, 12-16, 32, 33,
39, 40, 54, 81, 86, 126
responsibility, 7, 12, 13, 17, 31, 34,
38, 42, 60, 62, 63, 76, 82, 86, 87, 89,
90, 106, 135

school journeys, 22, 50, 66, 71, 101,
124
school practice, 53
Schools Council Report, 132
science, 24, 26, 32, 37, 41, 67, 70, 75,
76, 87, 88, 90, 96, 99, 106, 118, 121,
123, 132, 133, 136
seasonal topics, 109, 115
secondary school, 8, 55, 56, 57, 118,
133
self-appraisals, 134, 135
self-determination, 1, 7, 12
self-directed work, 7, 43
self-government, 7
sensori-motor intelligence, 52
sequential study, 109, 110
sequential work, 42, 110, 127
skills, 13, 19, 21, 26, 30, 31, 32, 37, 38,
41, 42, 44, 46, 50, 61, 62, 65, 66, 78,
79, 89, 91, 95, 97, 99, 100, 102, 106,
109, 110, 127, 130, 132, 133, 136
social change, 6, 8-11, 33, 48, 56, 76
social climate, 15, 45, 83, 84, 86, 88,
97, 99, 124, 126, 127
social development, 19, 31, 37, 55, 64,
65, 69, 72, 96, 133, 134
social studies, 111
social values, 50, 81-87, 115, 133
sociology, 2, 54, 56, 88, 89, 114, 126
space, 12, 17, 34, 43, 52, 61, 81, 91,
95, 96, 97, 99, 101, 110, 125, 129
specialists, 57, 101, 121, 125
speech, 22, 23, 25, 45, 109, 129

spelling, 102
staff meetings, 96
standards, 2, 3, 6, 12, 13, 14, 23, 47, 61, 81, 83, 100, 129, 130, 131, 132, 133, 136
statistical methods, 57
Stepney, 2
stereotypes, 78, 83, 84, 85, 87, 127
stories, 14, 17, 21, 37, 44, 45, 47, 50, 54, 69, 70, 71, 72, 73, 74, 75, 97, 101, 112, 125
streaming, 95, 125
subjects, 12, 37, 76, 94, 95, 98, 105, 106, 109, 121, 122, 123
survey of primary schools, 30, 129, 133, 140

TAMS tests, 26-30
tape recorder, 21, 26, 39
Taylor Report, 100
teacher, 1-4, 10, 12, 13, 15-18, 21-26, 31-35, 37, 38, 40-48, 50-54, 57-60, 62-64, 66-69, 72, 76-102, 105, 106, 108, 112-114, 120-130, 133-136
teacher education, 53, 135, 136
teaching, 4, 13, 16, 20, 31, 32, 37, 42, 44-46, 48, 51, 52, 56-59, 67, 79, 87-93, 97, 99, 101, 103, 111, 112, 121, 125, 127, 128, 130, 134, 135
teaching machine, 24, 39, 126
teaching style, 6, 30, 99
team teaching, 17, 32, 125
technological advance, 8, 33, 121
technological aids, 24, 39, 126

technology, 24, 70, 76
television, 8, 9, 24, 25, 26, 37, 39, 41, 43, 65, 66, 69, 114, 123
theory, 3, 10, 35, 41, 44, 45, 50, 53, 93
thinking, 13, 21, 26, 42, 46, 51, 52, 53, 58, 65, 68, 75, 77, 88, 89, 112, 129, 133
three Rs, 21
time, 17, 31, 34, 39, 40, 52, 61, 71, 88, 91, 96, 97, 99, 110, 111, 124
timetables, 11, 17, 79, 88, 97, 99, 104, 106, 124
tools, 43, 97, 114, 124
topical work, 102, 109, 111, 115, 127
traditions, 9, 11, 31, 42, 66, 82, 93, 114, 130, 131, 136
trial and error, 53

underachievement, 133
undifferentiated day, 17, 95, 96
urban society, 10, 22, 24, 76, 89

vandalism, 22, 59
vertical grouping, 19, 26, 32
video-tapes, 39
visitors, 23, 43, 62, 72, 125
visits, 37, 47, 66, 68, 75, 97, 101, 111, 115
vocabulary, 5, 102, 129, 134

waste material, 119, 120, 124
William Tyndale, 129, 130
writing, 21, 23, 43, 62, 75, 79, 94, 96, 102, 104, 108, 111, 113, 117, 125

The Harper Education Series has been designed to meet the needs of students following initial courses in teacher education at colleges and in University departments of education, as well as the interests of practising teachers.

All volumes in the series are based firmly in the practice of education and deal, in a multidisciplinary way, with practical classroom issues, school organisation and aspects of the curriculum.

Topics in the series are wide ranging, as the list of current titles indicates. In all cases the authors have set out to discuss current educational developments and show how practice is changing in the light of recent research and educational thinking. Theoretical discussions, supported by an examination of recent research and literature in the relevant fields, arise out of a consideration of classroom practice.

Care is taken to present specialist topics to the non-specialist reader in a style that is lucid and approachable. Extensive bibliographies are supplied to enable readers to pursue any given topic further.

Meriel Downey, General Editor

New titles in the Harper Education Series

Special Education: Policy, Practices and Social Issues edited by Len Barton, Westhill College, and S. Tomlinson, University of Lancaster

The Primary Curriculum by Geva M. Blenkin and A.V. Kelly, Goldsmith's College

Health Education in Schools edited by J. Cowley, K. David, The Health Education Council, and T. Williams, The Schools Council

Personal Values in Primary Education by Norman Kirby, Goldsmith's College

A Dictionary of Education by Derek Rowntree, The Open University

Teachers of Mathematics: Some aspects of Professional Life edited by Hilary Shuard, Homerton College, and Douglas Quadling, The Mathematical Education Trust

The following titles are published in association with the Open University Press

Discrimination and Disadvantage: The Experience of Ethnic Minorities in Employment edited by Peter Braham, Michael Pearn and Ed Rhodes

Social and Community Work in a Multi-Racial Society edited by Juliet Cheetham, Walter James, Martin Loney, Barbara Mayor and Bill Prescott

The School in a Multi-Cultural Society edited by R. Jeffcoate and Alan James